GROWING BY NUMBERS

How to scale up your small business with confidence

DELLA HUDSON FCA

The award-winning author of ***The Numbers Business***

Growing by Numbers
How to scale up your small business with confidence

ISBN 978-1-912300-32-7
eISBN 978-1-912300-33-4

Published in 2020 by SRA Books

A CIP record of this book is available from the British Library.

Printed in the UK

Dedication

To our dreams

To all those small business owners who put everything on the line to achieve their dream and to those who support us along the way.

To my children who have turned out better than I could ever have dreamed.

Contents

Foreword

Della describes this book as a road map and I truly believe road maps are an essential item for every entrepreneur! If you set a vision of where you want to go, it's pretty likely you'll need a map to get you there, and this book will help.

In these pages, Della showcases stories from clients she's helped and lessons she's personally learned along the way from scaling her own accountancy practice. In view of her background, of course Della highlights the importance of knowing your numbers, but there are also invaluable tips in here on everything from growing a team to introducing processes to drive up value in your business.

If you want to lead a well-run business, and potentially exit it too, this is the book for you.

Emma Jones MBE

Founder, Enterprise Nation

Introduction

You've successfully brought your business through the first few years as a start-up. You've learned from your mistakes and refined what you do so that you're ready to grow. Congratulations on making it this far.

Starting up takes a lot of energy from the founder but scaling up needs you to build a business that no longer requires you on a daily basis. You will probably be moving to the CEO role with a competent team taking care of the day-to-day operations. Your job is now as the captain of the ship.

Moving from the engine room to the bridge requires a change in approach from the initial firefighting and becomes much more strategic (although those fires may still flare up if they weren't fully extinguished in the first place). Scaling up isn't for everybody, so be clear on whether you want more income now, a bigger lump sum on retirement or a better work/life balance as there are often trade-offs to be made for you to get what you want.

Some of the things to consider include:

- Increasing the value of your business requires increasing profitability. There may be ways to do this other than by increasing turnover.
- Increasing profitability now can often be achieved by efficiencies rather than scale.
- Likewise, spending less of your time in the business can be achieved through increasing efficiency or reducing your current income and profits.
- A bigger team to cover holidays and sickness may take more of your management time.
- Finding your new role in the larger organisation may require a change of mindset from jack of all trades to master of one (which might not necessarily mean that you are the CEO).

This book will help you to review each section of your business and to make the necessary changes to help you move on up and, eventually, out when you're ready to retire and sell your creation. Knowing your exit plan will help you to decide which changes will be most beneficial for you.

Depending on the nature of your business, this might be about taking your turnover from £100,000 to £1m or £5m or beyond. These are the changes that are commonly required in all businesses. It's about taking the best of corporate methods and adapting them to a small business.

I keep a 'dreams and desires' file, an idea that I got from work that my father was doing with ex-drug addicts in Wiltshire. I think that it is very important to know what success looks like for you. Then you can set about achieving it through income from your business when trading but also on retirement. Another reason why it is useful to be clear what success means to you personally is because it is usually about more than just money. For one of my apprentices it was to drive a particular car. We established that he could already afford a second-hand version of this car which would fulfil his dream so he went ahead and bought one within a couple of weeks.

I love hearing how businesses started up in someone's garden shed or on the corner of their kitchen table. It is great to hear how entrepreneurs have taught themselves new skills as their business develops. I love helping those businesses to grow once the owners are in a position to bring in an expert from outside. I particularly like working with accountants but I like the variety of all sorts of businesses and 'borrowing' ideas from one industry to enhance another.

This book includes some of my own story and also those of my clients. These are all things which have worked in real life. But every business is different, so pick the ideas which you think will work in your own business. The rest may come in useful later.

This book is a road map that will help a competent business owner to:

- get a handle on the key numbers to improve in order to grow their business
- recruit and train a team
- create a highly systemised business, which can function independently of the business owner
- move from the kitchen table to external premises
- set up a marketing system that operates even during the busiest periods in order to grow the business organically
- keep an eye on the all-important cash
- decide how and when to pull in outside help
- run an ethical business, which contributes to the local community
- purchase a business
- sell a business.

Mine was an accountancy business, but I have spent my whole career running or advising a variety of other businesses too. This book provides you with one way to scale up your small business. Some things are common to all successful businesses but no two businesses are exactly the same. I'm sure that you can make plenty of your own mistakes, so please feel free to learn from mine.

Read the book straight through and then dip back into the chapters that are most relevant. And to provide a little extra help, there are free help sheets and videos on the Hudson Business website (www.hudsonbusiness.co.uk) and a list of further resources at the end of the book.

But above all, use the numbers in your business to track your progress as you work towards your goals.

Let's do better business.

Della Hudson FCA

Speaker, author and business coach

Top 50 Women in Finance (Accountancy Age, 2019)

Top 50 Women in Accounting (Practice Ignition, 2019)

Chapter 1

Understanding your accounts

1. Understanding your accounts

While much of this book talks about delegating I'm quite passionate about wanting business owners to understand their numbers. To know which numbers are good and which numbers need work. Because the numbers are the scoreboard for your business success.

The scoreboard

If you're into sport – I particularly like football, and I'm a Bristol City supporter – then you and your team are on the pitch working hard to score goals and achieve your dream. But it's not just the team, you also have your business coach there, who is advising and making sure that the team work in the best way possible. The coach can see how they can improve things because they have got the overall view from the bridge. He or she can see what's going on while the team are right in the thick of it.

As for the team manager, they couldn't be there without the team, and the team will do a lot better with a decent manager in place. In business it's good if you've got a coach, advisor or non-executive director (NED) helping you. You may well have an accountant who fulfils that function and that will really help you to make progress.

The problem with using accounts as your scoreboard is that it's all about numbers. And many people are actually terrified of numbers. I think that stems from school, because maths is one of the very few subjects where you either get it right or wrong. In the written subjects, yes you could probably do better, but it's very rarely wrong. Whereas with maths, it's very easy to see pages of corrections and feel intimidated.

But actually the numbers needn't be as terrifying as at school. So if you're one of the people who came out of school thinking 'I can't do maths, I can't do numbers', and therefore you're terrified of your accounts, don't worry. These days there is excellent software that does the really heavy lifting in producing your accounts, and the numbers are just patterns.

Pattern recognition

You don't need to track your numbers so much as the patterns. Are your numbers going up, or are they going down? Should they be going up or down?

Consider a sequence of playing cards. Most people recognise the patterns on playing cards and you can quickly spot the sequence. You can see which is the biggest and which is the smallest. You know whether they are going up, or if they are going down. You can see the patterns without thinking. We know these things instantly because playing cards are quite familiar and it's easy to see what they are.

You don't even have to count those numbers: you can see that a ten is higher than a two because the card is more crowded with hearts, diamonds, clubs or spades. It's just understanding patterns. We are good with patterns – the brain naturally recognises them; this is all a lot easier than pesky numbers.

If you are looking at a chart with your sales figures, you'd be really happy to see them going up. The software and your accountant work out the actual numbers; let them do the hard work. You just need to use the accounts.

When something isn't right

Sometimes, something isn't quite right. You can look at that pattern and you can see if a card is out of order or if it is the wrong suit. When you've got the same familiarity with your business numbers, you will be able to spot straight away when something is strange and needs a closer look. It's fairly straightforward: it's not rocket science and nor is 80 per cent of accountancy, so I want you to get in touch with that 80 per cent – leave the other 20 per cent to the numbers geeks and just stick with that 80 per cent that's really useful to you.

Who uses accounts?

Statutory accounts

These are the ones that your accountant completes for you at the end of the year in a specific format which is intended for certain users.

'The taxman'

HMRC of course needs a copy of them to check that your tax is correct so these statutory accounts are prepared in accordance with certain rules. For the most part these are logical and simple to follow, but there are some areas which are more complex. This is an area that accounting geeks love so that you don't have to.

Companies House

If you're a limited company, then a copy of your accounts is lodged in the public domain, so anyone can have a look at them. If you are a small company, with no more than around £10m turnover these days, then you submit filleted accounts, effectively a balance sheet and a few notes. This means that they're not that useful to outsiders, but they do give a bit of information.

Investors and banks

If you're looking for somebody to invest in your company *Dragon's Den* style, or a bank just for a loan or overdraft, they will ask for a copy of your accounts. They will also look at how up to date your accounts are, so if you're just meeting the annual deadlines by the skin of your teeth it may look as though you're not prioritising the finances of your business (and it would probably be true!).

Business managers

The managers in the business will want to see your accounts, your numbers, but actually they probably want more information than in the statutory accounts, because they are in a not very helpful format. I'll talk about what you really need in the next chapter.

Mortgage companies

If you own a small business, then a mortgage company will want to see the accounts for director–shareholders.

All sorts of people use your statutory accounts but the people who probably use them least are the company's own management.

You can read more in the next chapter or watch my Finance for Business Owners webinars (see Further resources).

Things to remember:

- The accounts are your scoreboard.
- If you're not comfortable with numbers then look for the patterns.
- Statutory accounts are designed for a variety of users but management accounts and key performance indicators (KPIs) are designed for you.

Chapter 2

Deciding your exit strategy

2. Deciding your exit strategy

Start with the end in mind

This chapter is about how you eventually retire from your business. It is included here as, although a lot of the actions are the same for running any successful business, there will be some differences based on how you intend to fund your retirement, when you expect to retire and what you will do with your time. Knowing your endpoint will enable you to focus on the key numbers throughout the lifetime of your business.

> **Clive's story***
>
> Clive contacted me for help preparing his professional services business so that, in five years' time, he could retire to the coast where he and his children could spend more time on the watersports and other activities they loved. After a couple of coaching sessions it became clear that Clive already had a business which he could operate remotely as his national and international clients were already used to dealing with him mainly via emails and online meetings. All work was either carried out by his remote team or outsourced overseas. At the time of writing Clive has put his house on the market and the family have already chosen the village and schools where they will live their new life. Clive will commute back to his old town just once a fortnight for any essential meetings.
>
> *(*All case studies are true but names have been changed to provide anonymity for the business owner)*

Issues to consider

There are several ways of generating a retirement fund from your business when the time comes. The best way for you will depend on the nature of your business and whether you wish to retire completely or just scale things back a little.

Some options are:

- Pay into a standard pension fund
- Pay into a SIPP (self-invested personal pension)
- Take cash out of your business to invest in property – residential or commercial

- Sell all or part of your business to a third party or to a management buyout (MBO)
- Work part time
- Franchise your business
- Put a manager into your business and step back

Pension funds

Let's deal with the conventional one first. Pension funds are a tax-efficient savings plan. You get tax relief on payments into the plan but you pay tax when you take it out in retirement, although usually at a lower rate because you are not earning so much. When you retire there are a variety of things that you can do with these funds to generate an income throughout your retirement.

Your pension is a tax-efficient way to pay yourself if you don't need the money today. It is also useful for pushing you back under certain thresholds so that you stay within a lower tax band or get to keep your child benefit.

If you are considering a pension fund then you should speak to a qualified independent financial advisor (IFA) on the best approach for your particular circumstances. They can also advise on SIPPs.

Property investment

You will pay tax on the cash you take out of the business to purchase all or part of your property.

A lot of people like to invest their spare cash in buy-to-let properties for income and capital gain. Remember that the increase in price of your additional property is taxable as a capital gain. HMRC is now checking the Land Registry to spot sales of properties that are not your principal primary residence (aka home).

With increases in stamp duty and the relief lost on mortgage interest, property is not such a tax-efficient investment as it used to be and you will need to make bigger gains through net rental income or capital gains on eventual sale.

Commercial property

Commercial property investments can be put into a SIPP and can be more tax efficient. If you own your own business premises then this is something that you could look into.

Sale of your business

You can sell your business to a third party or an MBO.

You can sell all or part of your business.

If you sell all of your business you may be able or even required to continue working at some level for a little while longer.

If you sell part of your business this will generate a lump sum that you can invest in any of the other schemes or spend it all on sweets.

Remember that in having a partner you will no longer have complete control of your company. A new owner or majority shareholder may take your business, which you have carefully built up, and do things that you do not agree with. Will they look after your customers? Your staff? Will you care? If you are selling a large proportion then you must be prepared for this. If you are selling just part of your business then don't forget to get a good shareholder agreement.

How to value your business

Ultimately your business is worth what somebody is prepared to pay for it. The valuation is often based on a multiple of the profit over the last three years although it will depend on your particular industry. There is more information on business valuations in Chapter 16. The profit is adjusted to include a market salary for businesses where the current owner usually takes a large chunk of their remuneration through dividends. There may also be other adjustments because the new owner will run the business differently, perhaps from cheaper premises or with fewer staff.

For accountants and other professional services businesses there is sometimes a clawback arrangement of some sort to take account of clients who move on because they do not feel tied to the business without you there or for any other reason. Similarly other businesses may have an element of the payment being dependent on future profitability. You can help by ensuring a good handover with knowledge transfer and introductions to key clients to take advantage of any personal loyalties. Once ownership transfers though you can only influence (if that) how the business is run.

You can arrange to sell the net assets of the business plus the goodwill/client list or you can sell the shares in your company. Your buyer may have a preference.

A buyer may be interested in your premises or they may wish to relocate your business.

You must also consider any staff. Will they transfer with the business or will you need to make them redundant prior to the sale? Do you have any strong feelings on this? If they transfer to the new owner along with the other assets of the business their employment rights will be protected under TUPE (Transfer of Undertakings Regulations).

Things that will increase the multiplier and hence the overall value of your business are systems. The better the business can run without you personally, the more valuable it will still be when you step out of the picture. Many of the things that you would do to franchise it also apply here (see below). Many of the things that you would do to help your business to run more efficiently, the type of things in this book, will also help to increase the final value of your business. If your business will run smoothly without you at the helm then it is a true business and not simply self-employment.

If you are thinking of selling your business then you should start preparing three to five years before sale. It may well be worth inviting a business advisor to come and give you the sort of independent review that you cannot carry out yourself.

You may even need a different structure for your business. The classic example is that accountancy practices and other professional services companies are sold based mainly on a factor of turnover, whereas they will probably have been run on a day-to-day basis to maximise your profit. Owner-managed businesses will have a lot of foibles according to what the owner values. For instance, we always used to support local grassroots sport through sponsorship. This was a combination of sponsorship and giving back to the community in a way that we could enjoy. Other owner-managed businesses might sponsor musical events and charities for much the same reason. As part of the pre-sale process it is worth reviewing every single cost to decide what it will offer, objectively, to a new owner.

As a majority shareholder working in the business, you will probably qualify for Entrepreneurs' Relief but do consider the tax position for silent partners. It is worth seeking tax advice early on in order to structure the sale, and the timing, for your benefit.

You also need to agree when you will be paid. All at once or over a couple of years?

Who accepts liability for previous debts or for rectifying poor work or faulty goods? Professional services businesses will need to provide up to six years' run-off insurance to cover any professional indemnity claims relating to work carried out under your supervision. This should cover all professional claims and protect you from personal liability. Other business owners should consider whether they are likely to require similar insurance.

How to increase the value of your business

- Systemise to make it less dependent on you and key staff in the event that they also leave.
- Systemise to maintain high quality/service levels.
- Make it less location dependent or move premises if these are not for sale.
- Increase profitability or turnover.
- Put procedures in an operating manual.

Management buyout (MBO)

This is similar to a third-party sale except that you will know that you have a good team to ensure that your clients and staff are looked after. This is a much simpler process but you may receive a lower price or payment over a longer period. This may be a buyout by all or part of the management team or it could include all employees through an employee ownership trust (EOT). This is not just a tax-efficient way of selling but it also creates a lasting legacy for current and future employees to own and enjoy. Did you know that all John Lewis/Waitrose employees actually own the company through an EOT? You can find out more in *The Eternal Business* by Chris Budd.

Working part time

You can scale back your business and just do the bits of work that you enjoy most, or for your selected clients. This will provide you with lower income but with more time. Your overheads may be disproportionately high. As with a start-up, you will still need to pay for full insurance, software licences and so on whether you use them full time or part time.

You may be able to sell the part of your business that you do not wish to keep or you could gradually run it down by reducing your marketing investment.

Franchising your business

This is best done with the help of a specialist to help you with standard systems, registering intellectual property, marketing to end users, marketing to franchisees, etc. You need to have something of value to franchisees that would save them time and cost compared to setting up their own business from scratch. A proven system of gaining and carrying out work is usually essential.

Employ a manager

With the right person to take care of the day-to-day running of the company you can dip in and out at your leisure. This will be easier if your business is heavily systemised. There's that word again!

You could outsource more and spend a proportion of your profits to buy yourself more time.

There are so many possible solutions and all of them will require some sort of preparation to get you the best deal. It is worth having at least some idea a long way beforehand of which way you hope to go so that you can structure your business or your pension plan or your property portfolio in plenty of time.

The numbers to watch

- Income requirements during retirement
- Time to retirement
- Expected length of retirement
- Valuation of business
- Valuation of pensions, investments and any properties which can be sold

Summary

- Work out where you want your business to be and by when, then decide what KPIs will drive your business forwards.
- Decide if you will fund your retirement out of the business income or whether your business can be sold to generate a lump sum.
- Measure these KPIs on at least a weekly basis; I had mine on a whiteboard in my office for all the team to see.
- Change your three to six main KPIs as you focus on improving different aspects of your business.
- Systemising your business is a worthwhile exercise in most cases. As well as increasing efficiency while you are running the business, it will make it easier to run part time, to franchise or to increase the value on sale.
- Documenting your systems will also help with most of these actions.
- Plan early so that you have time to save into a pension, extract cash in a tax-effective manner for investment elsewhere or to prepare the business for sale.
- Consider having a board, a business coach or similar for accountability as well as guidance.

Chapter 3

Your accounting toolbox

3. Your accounting toolbox

Running a business requires more than just statutory accounts once a year.

What you need in your toolbox:

- Strategic plan (your destination)
- Budgets (your planned route)
- Forecasts (your planned route revised for things that happen along the way)
- Actual monthly performance of all your KPIs
- Annual accounts (a summary of what happened last year)
- Comparison with previous years (are things getting better or worse?)
- Comparison with others in your industry
- Business valuation (your retirement fund)
- List of turnover and profit by customer to focus on those key to your business (and not to become overly dependent on them)
- Improvement plans
- Ideas – plenty of them

Planning and forecasting

When I set up my first business several years ago my business plan was little more than a few ideas and some estimated numbers, but in 2012, after getting fit and running the Bristol 10 km, I wrote what I called my Icarus Budget. As the name might suggest it was a huge aspiration and I blame the endorphin high. This was the five-year plan which turned my one-person band into a proper cloud accounting business. I've since made a point of writing my plans when I'm feeling at my most positive and then reviewing the actions at a later date to make sure that they are actually achievable.

We run free goal-setting webinars to help business owners to work out what they want from their own business. They can then join strategic planning days to put this into a proper business plan. (See Further resources.)

You need to know which direction you want your business to take in order to decide the actions to get you there. This requires some sort of a plan.

Your strategy will probably take a number of years so it is common to have a five-year plan. Five years is an arbitrary deadline but a convenient time horizon. How many of us, looking back five years, could have foreseen that we would be where we are today?

Set out what you want to achieve by the end of that time period. Start with the words and then break them down into numbers and actions.

I once hosted an interesting strategy day for a company with four director–shareholders who had been working together for years but were beginning to struggle. We quickly established that, between the four of them, they had three different objectives for the business so it was no wonder that they were all subtly pulling in different directions. We were able to come up with a strategy which satisfied two of the needs and part of the third so that everybody was happy and the business had clear direction. Once you know where you're going there is more chance that you will get there.

A detailed 12-month plan combined with the five-year plan is a good way to set this out. This should provide you with a course of action. The master plan is broken down into the actions needed to achieve the results and the key figures to check that you are carrying out those actions.

If you plan to achieve a certain amount of profit what does this mean in terms of sales and overheads? How will you achieve those sales? Who will be your customers? How much will they each buy? How will they know about you (marketing)?

As well as your financial plan you can see that you will need plans for marketing, sales and operation improvements/growth. Once you have detailed plans in place you need to be able to monitor them and this is where KPIs come in. Each month you need to sit down and compare your KPIs and financials with your plan to ensure that you are on track. If there are any shortfalls you need to understand what has happened and put together a plan to get back on track.

Spend time on the handful of KPIs which affect your business most. While my business was relatively cash rich, cash flow forecasting was not critical so I didn't spend time on this. I still believe that the most useful KPIs are those which monitor actions rather than results. You should still monitor the results of KPIs, of course, to ensure that they are the right actions.

Financial measures and ratios

The obvious figures to track are your turnover/income and profitability. You should also track these by customer/market/product so that you can focus on your most profitable areas.

Watch your mark-up and margin to ensure that you aren't selling at a loss. Take all your costs into account including import duty and delivery costs where appropriate. Track this overall and by customer/product/market. Don't forget to update it every time your prices or costs change.

Gross margin on a product is the profit you make after paying for the product and delivery. This is usually expressed as the percentage of profit over price.

Mark-up is the percentage that you increase the cost by to set your selling price. For instance, a teapot costing £4 and selling for £10 would have a gross profit of £6, a margin of 60 per cent and a mark-up of 150 per cent. The terms are often used interchangeably but they are all different. See Chapter 12 for more detail on these figures.

Cash is also key and there are a number of ways of measuring the liquidity of your business as well as the actual cash at the bank. Rather confusingly 'cash' is used to refer to money in the bank as well as petty cash.

Higher sales will increase your debtors (those who owe you money) so you need to track how quickly you are collecting that cash.

Debtor days is a common measure. This is the total sales (including VAT) divided by the outstanding debtors and then multiplied by 365. If your standard terms are 30 days from the end of the month then you would expect average debtor days of 45 as sales are invoiced throughout the month. If your standard terms are 30 days from invoice date then you would expect average debtor days of 30. This is something worth thinking about when setting your terms and conditions. You want your debtor days as low as possible so that the cash is in your bank sooner.

If you hold stock/inventory there is a trade-off between having sufficient stock available to sell and tying up money in stock. It may be worth using a slightly more expensive supplier if they can deliver faster. On the other hand, you may have larger customers who effectively want you to hold the stock on their behalf.

You can measure your **stock days** as the stock value divided by the cost of sales and multiplied by 365. Try to keep this as low as possible while still serving your customers.

You can measure your **stock turnover** as the cost of sales divided by the stock value. Try to keep this as high as possible while still providing a good customer experience.

Solvency

It is the legal responsibility of the directors to ensure that the business is not trading insolvently. This means that you should be able to meet all your debts as they fall due. Particularly sensitive debts are those owed to HMRC as VAT, PAYE/NI and corporation tax.

There are two main liquidity ratios that suppliers and banks will look at before extending you credit:

Your **current ratio** is the ratio of your current assets (stock + debtors + cash) to current creditors (those you owe payment to within the next year). This varies with industry but should usually be at least 2.

Your **quick ratio** is similar but excludes stock, which takes longer to convert into cash. The ratio is current assets excluding stock compared to current creditors. This also varies by industry but should usually be at least 1. (Again, see Chapter 12 for more on these terms.)

If your retirement plan involves selling your business then you will need to keep an eye on the value of your business. This will be a factor of turnover/profitability, goodwill/reputation, market share, net assets on your balance sheet and market conditions at the point you plan to sell.

The numbers to track:

- Sales (overall and by segment)
- Profit (overall and by segment)
- Your prices
- Your suppliers' prices
- Cash
- Debtors
- Debtor days
- Stock
- Stock days
- Stock turnover
- Liquidity ratios such as quick ratio and current ratio
- Market valuation of premises and other large assets
- Net assets (the figure at the bottom of your balance sheet)

You can't track all of these in real time so focus on three to six main KPIs on at least a weekly basis. I had mine on a whiteboard in my office for all the team to see. You can change these KPIs as you focus on improving different aspects of your business.

It also helps to work with a business coach or similar for accountability as well as guidance.

Engage your team in your business goals and celebrate your successes with them.

Chapter 4

Non-financial KPIs

4. Non-financial KPIs

Key performance indicators should be the object of your focus in order to drive your business forward. You will have certain KPIs for the company and more detailed ones for each department and even for each individual. You should have your KPIs at your fingertips.

Profit is the result of doing the right things. KPIs are a way of monitoring that you are doing those right things at an early stage. In this respect your KPIs are more important than your accounts as a management tool. Your KPIs, or the emphasis on different ones, may vary over time. For instance, as you gain more business you may move your focus from sales and marketing to efficiency and internal quality measures. It's no use continuing to improve your sales results if you're unable to process the resulting work to a sufficient standard.

If you're not sure where to start then your accountant or business coach may be able to help you to identify which KPIs are essential to your particular business, how to measure them and how to improve them.

Monitoring your marketing plan might involve KPIs such as:

- Number of flyers distributed or mailshots sent out.
- Speaking events. For professional services companies, speaking at more events will increase your profile and allow you to demonstrate your expertise.
- Regular social media posts. A great way of increasing your profile and networking with a wider range of people.
- Number of social media responses. You can look at the number of posts and then the response to those posts, be that in likes or in comments or people reading or sharing or tweeting it, whatever.
- Number of social media followers. It's not just the absolute number, it's the quality of those followers as well. When I was running my accountancy practice I sometimes chatted about football as well as business online. So I had all sorts of followers; the ones who were following me for football didn't help my business. Just having loads of followers isn't any good unless they are your target customers. It may be fun but don't lose sight of why you're doing your social media.
- RISE or similar score. This is an indication of your social media reach, and the extent that people are interacting with you and the content that you are posting. Rise.global is just one of the platforms that can measure the interactions and reach of your social media posts. Take this figure with a pinch of salt; it is easy to increase your score by posting pictures of cute puppies but this may not convert into enquiries.

- Number of enquiries and their source. This is to try to understand which of your marketing activities is most effective.
- Number of networking events. This increases your profile. One-to-one coffees are often much more productive than some of the larger events as you can make a quality connection rather than just collect business cards.
- Footfall: how many visitors there are to your premises.
- Number of blogs and articles written. These are another way of demonstrating your expertise and may be a better format for many or just a different format. Do try to avoid dry technical subjects which risk sending your readers to sleep. Food companies can share recipes for their products, etc. For me, the number of blogs I did was part of my marketing, so the more blogs I did meant that I was able to get more information out to more people. I used to try and do at least one blog per week. It depends how busy you are. You might aim to do one a week, three a week or just one a month. But whatever is right for you, you need to then make sure that you get that done.

Monitoring your sales plan for clients/customers could cover these sorts of KPIs:

- Number of appointments. If you sell sheds, you might find that appointments booked in your diary for people to see the sheds is better because you can just look at your diary and see 'Yep, it's full. That's good.' You don't even need to count. The diary is full. If it's a bit patchy, then it's not so good.
- Number of clients (with signed contracts). Or number of customers on your database or transactions per day/week/month. It is useful to track this as much of your admin cost is per customer, no matter whether they are large or small.
- Volumes of different products sold.
- Order size. Your average order size might be quite important, because if it takes you X amount of time and effort to get a sale, you want that sale to be as big as possible. It might be something that you want to practise – not selling to more people, but selling more to each of your customers. It's the classic McDonald's 'Would you like fries with that?' – when somebody comes in and orders a burger the staff have a script for trying to sell something extra at the same time, because they've already got them through the door.

Monitoring your efficiency/productivity

- Standardisation can reduce the number of different processes. For instance, accountants might measure the number of clients on their chosen software system.
- Number of jobs/orders outstanding. You will need to keep a pipeline of work. An architect will have a number of buildings waiting to be designed. An accountant will have the next set of books ready to complete the accounts when the current job is finished or if there is a pause due to a query. You will need to know the right level for your business. You want it high because you want to move straight on to the next task after you've finished the current job or if there is any delay, but you also don't want it to be too high because you know you'll have impatient clients out there waiting for their work to be done.
- Production time. How long does it take from the materials coming in the door to the widget coming off the production line? If you can speed up the production time then you can do more work in the same time. Which usually means more money coming in.
- Response time is useful for those repairing items or supporting IT systems. The faster you can respond to queries and then get them resolved means that you can invoice and receive payment faster. If you are on a retainer then it will be a measure of customer satisfaction.
- Time spent on different products or clients. I have two markets of accountants and other business owners. I also like to see the sales and costs of my books, my online courses, my coaching and my speaking. I also track the time spent on each of my markets and products/services because time is a limited resource.
- Chargeable hours. A lot of other professional services firms record their time spent on client work that directly generates profit and how much is just spent on admin, marketing and other support functions. You may be able to increase your time spent on profitable activities if you invest in automating some of the support activities.
- Rework is a useful quality measure. How many items need to be redone? For example, a circuit breaker that's failed as it has come off the production line (or, even worse, when it gets out to the customer on site), a mistake in a set of accounts when you come to review them before sending out to the client. Anything that is not right first time is costing your business, because it needs to go back and be reworked. Quality saves money. All your quality statistics should be quite important to you.

Monitoring your financial plan

- Work in progress (WIP)/debtors (also known as lockup). Some of your cash is tied up in uninvoiced work and unpaid bills. If you read Chapter 14, 'Controlling your cash flow', you will see that, with fixed fees paid in advance, it is possible to have 'negative work in progress'.
- Profit and cash in bank, although these figures are the result of getting the other indicators right.
- Number of clients on direct debit.
- Profitability of different products. Construction companies might have sales of labour and sales of parts that they want to separate out. They almost certainly want to record their hours spent on each job.

As you can see, many of these KPIs aren't directly financial but, if you get these right, the financial figures will look better. Even if you are terrified of your accounts you may know these numbers off the top of your head. I have a client who wholesales welding gas. At any time of the month they know exactly how many cylinders they have sold this month and can immediately compare that to last month and last year. Although the prices vary with the exact product it is clear that more cylinders is better.

Monitoring your impact on the world

- Carbon footprint. It is becoming increasingly important to monitor the carbon footprint of all that we do and businesses should be no different. You may be able to make small or large changes to reduce your footprint or to offset it by donating to one of the groups which plant a comparable number of trees.
- Staff happiness. There are a number of measures in this area but the idea is to keep happiness as high as possible to reduce staff turnover and increase productivity. A happy team will be more productive but does that mean installing a pool table, providing free fruit or just allowing time off for a sick child?
- Net promoter score. This is one of many measures of customer satisfaction. How likely are they to recommend you to others?

As you can see there are all sorts of non-financial indicators and, depending on your business, there could be plenty of others that are useful to you. Your accountant or business coach should be able to help you to work out which numbers are your KPIs and are both useful and simple to monitor.

Useful numbers

- Time spent
- Order size
- Production time
- Number of appointments
- Percentage or time for rework
- Blogs and articles published
- Social media performance
- Outstanding jobs waiting to be done
- Chargeable hours
- Carbon footprint
- Happiness
- Net promotor score

Summary

There is more to measure than just your financial numbers. Focus on what you can do early on to improve your financial impact. Consider:

- Marketing work and return
- Sales
- Efficiency and productivity
- World/community benefits

Chapter 5

Setting your prices

5. Setting your prices

Your business needs to make a certain amount of money to cover direct costs, wages, other overheads and an amount for you. Even a charity needs to cover costs. Your personal profit target is probably more than you would want for the same number of hours as an employee as you are bearing all sorts of additional risks beyond those of a normal nine to five with a guaranteed pay cheque.

Pros of proper pricing

The income that you generate in your own business brings you these benefits:

- Financial freedom is the obvious one. If you were to replace yourself with an employee doing the same work at a commercial salary would there still be any profit? If not, this is self-employment rather than a business. It may be that self-employment is all that you want or it may be a step on the way to growing an independent business. There was a point when I was in this situation too on the way to scaling my business. Earning money for ourselves is usually a major motivation in setting up a business, so let's do it well.
- Quality and pride. If you want to provide a service or product of which you can be proud then you need to be able to spend sufficient time to put in the work required. Do you feel as though all the work you produce is top quality? How often do you rush to complete a job because it is just haemorrhaging cash and time? Only do work that you can be pleased to acknowledge as your own.
- Time freedom. If you do not charge enough to pay someone to do the work it is often the business owner who puts in the extra hours to complete the job. Proper pricing will pay for time, either personal time or time to grow your business.
- Covering your growing salary and overhead bills. Hopefully you have allowed for this from the start. If you set up with the 'I'm working from home with no costs' type of prices then you may find that you need to spend time replacing all your customers with those who pay full price before you can start to scale up.

Cons of proper pricing

- Losing clients who can't or won't pay the necessary fee.

Issues to consider

- Market price and where you sit in the market
- Value to your client
- Cost to you (including a share of overheads and your own profit element)
- How to increase your prices

Price and your competitors

When you first set up in business you usually set your price somewhere in line with your competitors as if this is the market price for the service that you provide without differentiating yourself to justify a different price.

Cost-based pricing is normal in retail where products are bought in at one price and then sold on for the cost plus a percentage mark-up.

This used to be normal for professional services such as the hourly charging of traditional accountants and solicitors with no reward for efficiency or automation. Carrying out a similar job will be faster the second time so it would be unfair to penalise one client for your learning curve or to undercharge another. More professionals are now moving to fixed fees to remove the uncertainty for clients. These fixed fees are usually based loosely on the expected number of hours.

Value pricing is when you set your prices on the value of the benefit to your customer. If a boiler fails in the middle of winter then the acceptable price of installing a new boiler will be significantly higher than in the summer.

One thing that is clear is that you cannot compete on price against the big corporations that 'pile them high and sell them cheap'. These companies have purchasing power and economies of scale which you cannot hope to match. Also, you probably can't compete with the smallest businesses and the gig economy based at home with minimal overheads. Competitor businesses below the VAT threshold can sell to the public or non-VAT-registered clients who cannot reclaim VAT without the 20 per cent VAT premium.

Price and quality

What you can compete on is quality or value for money.

Thinking of your typical client and how long it takes you to do a fairly standard job of average quality, how much would you charge for that particular job?

Now consider how much more it would take to provide a 'Wow!' kind of job. How much could you charge? How much extra would it cost? How would people compare this with your competitors?

When new clients came to me and complained that they were not getting the kind of service that they wanted from their accountant, the first thing I did was to ask how much they were paying. My response was usually along the lines of 'How can you expect the service that you describe for that fee?'

It is rare to get extraordinary value at the cheap end of the market. The most extreme example was somebody who was paying £50 a year to a family friend and expected monthly management accounts for that price. A job that I would price at a few thousand pounds! As she was a small one-person band, that price was not realistic for her but neither was her need for monthly accounts. We agreed on a realistic price and service for her business and told her which key numbers to monitor each month.

If new prospects generally got along with their accountant but felt that they weren't getting what they wanted from them, I would usually suggest that they negotiate a different service and probably a higher fee. Some still preferred to come to us as they felt that their accountant couldn't provide the required service. This is a warning to make sure that existing clients know all the services that you offer so that they don't need to start looking elsewhere.

Even with something as simple as conveyancing, which is a fairly standard job and, on the face of it, doesn't need a qualified solicitor, you might benefit from paying a little more. We bought a bog-standard ten-year-old estate house without a mortgage so we decided to use one of the cheap conveyancing firms. When we came to sell we used a proper solicitor as the matter was more complex because we were buying another property and there was a mortgage involved. We discovered that our buyers' solicitors were much more thorough than our original conveyancers had been. We ended up having to pay for insurance as there was information that we were unable to provide because our original conveyancer had never requested it from our original vendors.

Increasing your prices

Even in retail, if you can add value in some way, you can often charge a premium. Consider the price you would pay for a basket of toiletries beautifully packaged as a gift compared with the price you would pay for almost identical toiletries sold separately and purchased as part of your weekly shop. (Adding value yourself is also a good hint for Christmas presents when you're feeling hard up.)

Many people worry that by putting up their prices they may lose business, but let me show you an example.

If you have 100 sales of £1,000 each and an associated cost of £500 (so £500 profit) you might choose to increase your prices by 10 per cent to £1,100.

Now, instead of an income of £100,000 and a profit of £50,000 you would have income of £110,000 and profit of £60,000.

If you lose 10 per cent of your clients through this 10 per cent price increase you would have 90 clients paying £1,100 each and so an income of £99,000 and a profit of £54,000. You have increased your profit by £4,000 while having more time to do a good job for fewer clients.

With this example you could afford to lose 17 per cent of your customers and still make the same profit but you would be ahead on the processing costs because you are handling fewer transactions.

As an added bonus your most price-sensitive customers are probably those who cause you the most trouble. You probably have your own example of where you have been squeezed on profit and the client was still not satisfied.

Negotiating prices

When you first set up in business you are often feeling your way on pricing. After a while you know what you are worth, although people sometimes still try to negotiate beyond this.

You could have your starting prices on your website, or at least a printed price list for your own reference so that you do not quote unrealistic prices when put on the spot.

It also helps to package your services. Clients can choose the service package that suits them but the price for each package is fixed. When I have been asked for a cheaper price I have helped the client to decide what they can do for themselves to reduce their costs, such as some basic bookkeeping. If they do not wish to change the services then I have to explain that the team is unable to provide a level of service that we can be proud of for any less. Sometimes I have to let prospective clients go because we cannot do what they want to a satisfactory standard for the fee that they can afford. There are plenty of other accountants out there and I've sometimes even been able to refer business to my competitors.

Turning away the wrong business

If you find that you have a lot of enquiries from clients who are not right for you, then it is worth building relationships with others who may be looking for exactly that type of business. For instance I did not take on new clients who had left things until the last minute. If clients cannot prioritise their accountancy then they are depriving themselves of an essential tool to grow their business. Our expertise was helping businesses to grow: we couldn't do it for them if they were not serious about their own business.

Of course I made an exception for a client who was late because he had been diagnosed with cancer and the team and I pulled out all the stops to ensure that everything was completed on time so that he did not incur penalties.

Deciding your price

So, how do you determine what your services are worth?

I once wrote a single letter to HMRC which took no particular research and saved a client £2,400 in tax. The admin that I had to complete, in line with the Institute of Chartered Accountants in England and Wales (ICAEW) guidelines, in order to take on the client actually took longer than writing the letter.

So what do you think I should have charged?

a) £100 as the notional cost of my time to write the letter.

b) £300 as the cost of my time to speak to the client, carry out all the necessary new client admin including money-laundering checks for HMRC and then the time to write the actual letter (this was a one-off piece of work).

c) £800 as the client would still be better off by £1,600 if the appeal was successful.

d) Not a fixed fee but 50 per cent of any tax saving.

Was the client paying for my time or my expert qualification and 20+ years of experience that allowed me to write the short letter? I decided that he was paying for my expertise and charged accordingly.

Why do professionals and tradespeople charge by the hour? It's usually because they have always done it that way but, if it's a fairly standard job (obviously this doesn't apply to every job) where they know roughly the time it will take, then it gives the customer more certainty if they are quoted a fixed fee rather than an hourly rate.

Think about how you set your fees.

Presenting your prices

There has been a great deal of research showing that if you present three models of increasing price and quality, people will often avoid the cheapest as they do not wish to be seen as 'cheap'.

You could have bronze, silver and gold packages. Or perhaps something a little more creative as long as there is an indication of an increase in value along with the increase in prices.

Warning

If you increase your prices without giving value for money then you will end up losing business and reputation, so do not promise what you cannot fulfil.

Also, any plumbers charging too much of a premium during the busy winter period, for example, may find that they're not called in for the annual maintenance or anything else.

My favourite client reference was: 'You are more expensive than [another local accountant] but much easier to deal with.'

I like it because it shows that I got our pricing right on this one and the client appreciated that we were giving value for money. I used this quote in our marketing for a while.

Annual increases

Don't forget that your costs are going up and that your clients' businesses are growing and changing too. Make time to review your client list each year to ensure that everybody is receiving the services that they need and discuss additional (or no longer necessary) services with your client. You should also have a standard inflationary increase to cover your own costs and it is worth having this included in your engagement letter.

Plumbing businesses can go back through all their call-outs to schedule maintenance visits over the quieter summer period.

Overcharging or underservicing?

Have you ever been sitting in a restaurant waiting for your meal and fancied another drink? This happened to me recently and the server was nowhere to be seen, so I was left sitting, thirsty and noticing the lack of service and the long wait for food.

Although it may sometimes be irritating to be cross-sold extras, it was probably more infuriating to be without the drink that I wanted, which also led me to notice faults that I would otherwise have overlooked. As well as losing out on about 21 per cent extra sales, the restaurant had an unhappy customer who may well go elsewhere next time.

You don't need a hard sell but do ensure that clients are aware of additional services that you think may be of use to them.

How to get rid of unprofitable customers

Once a year it is a good idea to evaluate your customers. If appropriate, do this with your team too. Clients who were right for us when I first started out were no longer our ideal clients as we grew because of the disproportionate amount of admin associated with maintaining a client, no matter how big or small.

We would get the team together and sort them into:

A. The perfect client, profitable and easy to work with as a business and as people.

B. Pretty good clients, for the same reasons.

C. Not quite there but, with a bit of work, they would be A or B clients. This might mean tightening up on how we carried out their work, or training them to provide information more promptly or adjusting their fees to reflect the work we were now doing.

D. Didn't suit our current profile. Perhaps they were lovely people but unprofitable clients and increasing their fees wouldn't provide them with sufficient value. Sometimes they were disorganised, which could be resolved if they took on a competent bookkeeper. Anybody who was unpleasant to me or my team was also on this list if they hadn't been dropped already.

It would then be the account manager's job to make the changes to improve our C clients. It was my job to improve or move on the D clients as professionally as possible, preferably to another accountant more suited to their needs and budget. We would make sure that this transfer went as smoothly as possible; after all, it was us who had changed rather than them.

Avoiding pitfalls

If you are worried about a generic price increase or don't know what you're worth, then you can phase in an increase by starting with new clients. Then just increase prices for a few existing clients each month.

Don't be afraid of losing poor clients.

Sam's story

Sam runs a property management company. When I was first called in he was working long hours, seven days a week. He was aware, in theory, of the need to move on unprofitable clients but not quite sure how to do it professionally. Here's the process we went through:

- His financial controller provided an analysis of the criteria for a profitable client so we were able to come up with the list quite objectively.
- We discussed how his business had moved on and why they were no longer able to look after these clients profitably if they wanted to provide their usual high levels of service.
- We came up with a script that he could use as a basis for the individual conversations.
- Where possible he identified agents who would provide the basic service at an affordable price.
- He contacted each client and explained that the business was no longer able to provide them with a quality service at an affordable price and made the introduction to the new agent.

As a result the business lost 22 per cent of their work, which freed up a lot of Sam's time. They also lost 6 per cent of their profit but Sam quickly replaced this because he now had time to manage the enquiries from ideal clients.

The numbers to watch

- The criteria/size of your ideal client
- Set a minimum fee if appropriate
- Average income per client/product
- Profitability per client/product/geographic market

Summary

- You are in business to make money not to provide a charitable service.
- There is nothing wrong with being paid what you are worth.
- Charge enough to provide the level of service that your client expects and deserves.
- Quality commands a higher fee but do make sure that you fulfil your promises.
- Try bundling your services into packages.
- Increase all your fees annually.
- Don't be afraid to increase your fees if they are too low.

Chapter 6

Budgeting and controlling costs

6. Budgeting and controlling costs

My background includes working as a financial controller in large companies and I am a great believer in cost control rather than blind cost-cutting.

There are times when it is right to go through a bootstrapping period, when your money is constrained and you invest time instead, for instance in the start-up phase. Bootstrapping involves putting in extra time and effort in order to save paying for something or somebody to do the work. This works as you have more time because you have fewer customers to service. Once your time has become a precious commodity, you need to take a fresh look and see what it will really take to grow your business. I don't want you to waste your money but I do know that one way to pretty much guarantee a business failure is to stop investing in it.

As a scale-up it is important that standards do not drop for your existing customers while you allocate money, time and resources to other areas. If appropriate you may decide to seek finance for your expansion.

Cost control

This is about spending money as an investment in the growth of your company. It might be paying for software to reduce time-consuming manual processes. The focus is on value, not absolute cost.

Cost reduction aka bootstrapping

This is about cutting spending to the bare minimum. It is about making do with what you can afford now, although you may end up paying more at a future date to replace or upgrade.

I went from a DIY website to a £500 site to a £3,000 site. I believe that each was worth the money that I spent but, by starting out with a DIY site, I learned a few new skills and was able to save cash for things that I couldn't do at all. This was not a productive use of time but time was not the most limited resource at first. It was also a good learning experience.

A downside of this cost-cutting mentality is that business founders often get into the habit of doing things themselves instead of paying an expert to do it for them cheaper, faster and/or better. This is why many business owners still find themselves working 80-hour weeks after the initial start-up period is over: because they 'can't afford' to hire somebody else to do it.

Here are a few ideas on controlling your costs.

People costs

- Recruit a part-timer.
- Recruit somebody junior and cheap who will take more time.
- Recruit somebody senior who can do the job fast and well even though their hourly rate may be higher.
- Recruit temporary staff for different projects as you grow.
- Outsource the activity. This flexibility works well for a company which is in transition or scale-up mode. The skills which you need in each phase may be different so you are only paying for exactly what you need at each stage.

Recruit for the work that you need and don't be obsessed with padding it out to provide a full-time role which might require two or three different skill sets. There are all sorts of reasons that people might be looking for part-time work. In my experience the school gates are thronged by highly qualified mothers (mainly) who would kill for a job that used their skills and still allowed them to be available for their children. Our local post office employed two mothers who were economics and marketing graduates and my old cleaner had a Master of Business Administration (MBA). You could be employing one of these for a few hours a week or even a month. This is ideal for smaller companies which can't afford to pay for the level of expertise that they need, and don't have the need for a full-time person in this role. It isn't just mothers who need this flexibility so keep an open mind.

You can provide flexibility in hours but, in many businesses, also in location. Right from the start we ran on a remote desktop so our team could work from anywhere in the world provided there was an Internet connection. Although all our staff were office based it meant that they could work through snow, floods, vague delivery times and children's illnesses or even because they wanted to be at home with a new puppy.

Talking of which, we used to have dogs in the office (once the puppy was house-trained!). These are little things that make people happy and don't actually cost you any money. If you can't trust your team to work unsupervised at least part of the time, then I would question whether they are the right people for your business.

Another way to get flexibility is to outsource. I have used a virtual PA where I only paid for the hours worked. We used an outsourced answering service to cover when our team were out of the office, in meetings or on the phone. Naturally clients used us to outsource their bookkeeping and payroll so that they could focus on what they were best at. We could do the same work better and faster than most of them. You will often find this when you delegate to experts. This is one of the reasons that I opted for a hosted desktop; it was backed up, kept secure and maintained by experts, leaving me free to do what I was best at, which was growing my business and helping clients to do the same.

An obvious thing is to outsource your bookkeeping to somebody who can do it faster *and* better, which may even save you some money.

The key to using human resources internally or externally is to organise your business into systems.

1. Identify your systems, starting with the most repetitive.
2. Write down the procedure.
3. Can you simplify it?
4. Can you automate it?
5. Can you delegate it to someone cheaper or more expert?

Consider temporary staff for project work or to help you during busy periods, rather than keeping a larger permanent workforce. Zero-hours contracts have been abused by some larger businesses but they are a good alternative for regular temps, giving them employment rights that they would not have otherwise.

Premises costs

For many people, premises is a large part of their overhead budget. Leases can seem very inflexible for a rapidly expanding business. If you're going to double your workforce in three to five years, then do you want to pay today for the bigger offices to save the hassle of moving to larger premises at a later date?

Again, for growing businesses, flexibility is the key. Serviced offices are ideal as you can swiftly move into a small office with instant utilities, Internet and telecoms infrastructure. The most common of these are Regus and WeWork but there are also many independents that can offer a better service or price.

As your business grows you can take on a second office in the same building, have two smaller offices opened out into one or move along the corridor without changing address. This is, of course, subject to your building having sufficient growing-on space available at the same time that you need it, so do think ahead.

Serviced offices can also provide a full-time receptionist, photocopiers, printers and PA services at an additional cost.

In my region we have identified a lack of 'grow-on' space and are working with the local councils and landlords to create more facilities.

Don't forget that if you decide to purchase your own commercial premises, these can be wrapped up in a tax-efficient SIPP to provide the business owner with a future pension.

Marketing: investment or overhead?

Marketing is often a large budget item for a growing business. This is where it pays to use an expert to help you put the right strategy in place.

Marketing is shown as an overhead but do record how effective each campaign and method is for you. Things like social media can appear to be free but are actually quite time consuming to get the best out of them, so do value your time as this becomes more limited. Bootstrappers (start-ups with minimal resources) need to invest time in marketing to make up for their lack of cash.

Different types of marketing will have different times to return a benefit and, as a new business, it is best to invest in a mixture to generate clients now and in the future.

You can find marketing consultants to advise you on what will be most effective for your business and its aims, and you can find experts who will actually run the campaigns for you. I used a mixture of my own copy as well as buying in some material because I didn't have the time to generate enough content myself. I now write copy for busy accountants, bookkeepers and fintech businesses.

Web content needs to be original for search engine optimisation (SEO) purposes so I have always written this myself. I can't add value to a tax card full of numbers so I just pay somebody else to produce this for me, just as I pay somebody to write and maintain our tax app. I don't have time to learn more technology when I'm busy keeping up with constantly changing tax and company law.

Technology

This brings us on to IT, where there are many decisions to be made.

IT decision 1 – automated or manual?

I describe myself as a competent user and I spent three years supporting and maintaining the accounting systems at National Grid. If I had all the time in the world I could have learned about each of our systems in depth and maintained them myself but my business was accountancy, not getting bogged down in the nitty-gritty of servers and coding websites. We were in the business of helping businesses to grow, so spending my time with my nose under the bonnet of a computer would not have helped my clients.

In my bootstrapping days I did tax calculations on spreadsheets that I had written myself. With hindsight, even then I should have purchased tax software so that I could spend more time adding value for clients. I would always recommend automating repetitive or complex jobs so that you work on that which only you can do. See Chapter 7, 'Establishing your systems and services', for more ideas. The time saved for you to focus on your business will pay for itself in results elsewhere.

IT decision 2 – integrated or stand alone?

Do you buy software separately for each part of your work or do you buy a single integrated package? Xero and QuickBooks Online (QBO) are bookkeeping software which connects to all sorts of other business systems such as the software you use for your tills, stock, customer relationship management (CRM), estimating/quoting jobs, tracking time or website sales.

If they don't talk to each other through an API (application programming interface, software which enables different apps to access each other's data) then it may be possible to use something like Zapier or Workato to save rekeying information.

There is a time saving in having software packages which talk to each other in this way. The more you scale up your business, the more time this will save.

IT decision 3 – market leader or cheaper?

Our business had standardised on Microsoft Office but I know others who prefer OpenOffice as a money-saving exercise in spite of the inefficiencies. (There is a time cost in making this less-well-known software integrate with some systems.)

IT decision 4 – cloud or server?

We used cloud-based software wherever available and a hosted desktop for everything else. Our server was somewhere in the country with a failsafe elsewhere. We paid a monthly fee for the server and an expert team to maintain it. We did not have the huge capital outlay to purchase our own server and back-up server and did not need to worry about when to replace them. We didn't need to worry about software upgrades, back-ups or security. Having worked in disaster recovery I was quite happy to let the experts deal with this.

If our Internet connection failed for any reason then we had the option of working elsewhere. As our PCs were dumb terminals (you may remember these if you've used an old mainframe) there was no data lost if somebody stole one.

This is the reason that we usually recommended Xero software for clients who use their own bookkeeper. This is cloud-based software that can be accessed from anywhere and you can invoice, log expenses and log time from your smartphone while out and about. We worked with all sorts of cloud software, including QBO, Receipt Bank and the more common Office 365 with OneDrive.

IT decision 5 – software or you?

We had workflow software to track jobs through the business. The idea of our workflow software was that anyone could see what was happening with any client at any point in time. It made me replaceable, as basic knowledge was not held in my head. If your business runs independently of the owner it is a saleable commodity and can be part of your pension plan.

CRM software involves much the same idea. It takes the business out of your head and into a system that the whole team can use. There are some relatively cheap, cloud-based options out there and now is probably the time to move on from the free versions with limited functionality.

IT essential: disaster recovery

On the subject of disaster recovery I strongly suggest that you write out your contingency plan in the event that your PC becomes corrupted or stolen, or your Internet connection or telecoms fail. We kept a paper list of all IT and communications contacts on the office wall as it would be no good held electronically if the system had failed.

If you are dependent on your PCs, then I recommend looking into a maintenance contract that will cover you for emergency work or for routine upgrades and other odd problems. You can opt for an ongoing contract or pay as you go. The latter will be more expensive but you only pay when you have a problem.

Compliance

You should, by now, have all the basics in place but it is worth checking that you haven't missed anything before you put your head above the parapet as a growing business:

- Have you got all your necessary licences in place to trade?
- Have you got planning permission for all building work and signage?
- Do you have contracts and work permits for all staff?
- Do you have PRS for Music (formerly the Performing Right Society) licences for music that your staff listen to in the workplace? Or a TV licence for your reception area or the staff room?
- Are all your risk assessments and fire assessments up to date?

Avoiding pitfalls

If you cut costs too far the business will be unable to function and so will fail.

There is an opportunity cost to bootstrapping. You may not be able to take advantage of an opportunity if you do not have sufficient funds to invest. In other words 'you have to be in it to win it'.

There is also a cost involved in shopping around to save pennies when you could be earning far more out there doing what you are best at.

Selling through third-party sites

It is common to start up as an Internet retailer through a third party such as Amazon, eBay or Etsy. By now you will be paying the commercial rates for your listings and payments so it may be worth adding an online shop to your own website. This is particularly useful if you have repeat customers as you can invite them to your own shop once they have made their initial purchase through Amazon, etc.

Outsourcing fulfilment

You may be starting to consider your own warehouse and delivery fleet but, until then, you can outsource your fulfilment to a company such as Amazon. You will pay for storage, order processing, returns and delivery.

The numbers to watch

- Turnover per FTE (full-time equivalent) employee
- Costs as a percentage of turnover
- Costs compared to budget or previous years
- Summary of flexible options for a growing business
- Part-time staff
- Temporary staff
- Outsourcing
- Serviced offices
- Lease rather than buy premises
- Lease rather than buy vehicles and equipment
- Software as a service
- Third-party sales sites
- Outsourced fulfilment

Summary

- An expert should be able to do things cheaper, faster and/or better than you can.
- Consider part-time or outsourced help.
- Consider different ways of paying for technology up front or as a service.
- Consider pay-as-you-go versus maintenance contracts.
- Please consider all your overheads as an investment as well as a cost.

Chapter 7
Reviewing your systems and services

7. Reviewing your systems and services

Hopefully you've been creating systems for all the regular processes within your business from day one. These can start out as checklists and templates, which become proper procedures as you begin to take on staff. The procedures will constantly evolve as your business grows and you discover better ways of doing things. In a growing business your written procedures will need constant review if they are to reflect what is actually happening for more than a few months at a time.

Pros of systemising

Systemising your business will give you some or all of the following benefits. It will:

- make it easy to carry out work to a similar (high) standard each time
- make it easier to train employees
- make it easier to delegate to your existing team
- make it easier to automate processes
- make the business less dependent on you so that it is more saleable
- enable you to take a holiday with confidence
- allow you to carry out more work in the same time as you don't need to reinvent the wheel each time, therefore increasing profits.

Cons of systemising

There are no real cons to having a properly systemised business apart from the time it takes to keep documentation up to date.

Jobs that you can systemise

- Professional services: common pieces of work from initial briefing to sign off and invoice, booking travel, expenses claims, leave requests, recruitment and training, and for onboarding new clients
- Shops: cashing up, locking up, stocktaking, reordering, dealing with customer returns, banking cash (or moving to cashless systems)
- Restaurants: food handling, laying up, meet and greet, dealing with delays and other complaint handling, food ordering and stock control
- Trades: answering phones and taking messages, handling client enquiries, diary booking, quotes and invoices, chasing payment
- Marketing
- Template letters, emails and contracts

How can you systemise?

1. Read Michael Gerber's *E-Myth* book for a detailed method (see Further resources).
2. The Pareto Principle, sometimes known as the 80:20 rule, suggests that 80 per cent of the profits come from 20 per cent of the products/customers. Similarly that 20 per cent of processes control 80 per cent of your work. This means that you should focus on those core processes first: those which support the majority of the customers or products. Getting these right will have most impact on the efficiency and profitability of your business.
3. Map out the process with wallpaper, or rolls of drawing paper and sticky notes. There are online tools to do this but this way it is easy to see and share with a small team around a table. Sticky notes can be moved around as you start to fill in more detail about the existing system.
4. Write this up as the existing procedure, warts and all, so that you have a base that (sort of) works.
5. Now repeat the mapping and include any improvements. Seek to make the processes more efficient and to eliminate rework or poor customer service which leads to costly (time or money) rectification.
6. Write up this improved procedure.
7. Complete the task yourself by only following the procedure.
8. Add whatever extras you need.
9. Get somebody else to complete the task by following the procedure.
10. Add whatever extras you need.
11. Review the process regularly to:

- Make sure that it is working
- Add any variations that you hadn't originally identified
- Eliminate bottlenecks
- Improve your processes.

12. Quality should be a process of continuous improvement: go back and repeat the cycle above on a regular basis.

The checklists which might have served you initially now need to be developed into procedures which can be used for training employees. As you move from delegating individual jobs to handing over whole areas of workflow these procedures will ensure that you can preserve consistency and quality.

As this is a continuous improvement process we might, for example, discuss ways to improve a particular process internally or how we could provide more value for our clients. In our case we also kept improving our workflow software.

By the time I sold the business my role was almost entirely business development and business advice. This was by virtue of my qualifications and my experience running Hudsons and larger businesses prior to that. The next step would have been to recruit another business advisor who could have taken on this element of my role by following and improving my systems.

So that's how we automated, delegated and generally systemised our business, and I loved helping clients to improve theirs too.

Sam's story

Sam runs a residential property management company (see p.43). He had successfully recruited a competent team and they were capable of handling more but he was often the bottleneck because they needed his expertise. We switched Sam's focus away from doing the work himself to spending slightly longer writing more 'how to' guides on the common issues. Soon the team were starting to write their own 'how to' guides. As each person found a better way of doing part of the job they shared it with the team.

Who can help?

See Further resources for useful software.

We also provide coaching, training and retreats for business owners.

You might use an independent consultant to help map and improve your processes, or as a facilitator in the mapping, a source of new ideas and an extra pair of hands.

Matthew's story

Matthew runs an accountancy business. His aim is to work himself out of the business ready for retirement so we looked for areas where he was a bottleneck. Invoicing was one of those areas because he was the only one who knew what needed to be invoiced. We agreed that:

- All annual fees would be subject to the same annual percentage increase so that the team could raise draft invoices.
- With a known fixed fee, clients could spread the payment over 12 months, which was easier for both their cash flow and for Matthew's.
- Any ad hoc work would be invoiced as it was completed rather than added to the annual bill so that there would be less chance of a client querying this and so, not only would it be invoiced sooner, but there would be fewer queries so it would be paid faster.
- Clients would be encouraged to pay by direct debit to reduce admin costs for the client and Matthew.

Avoiding pitfalls

It could become a full-time role documenting the ever-changing systems in a growing business, but the important thing is to communicate with your team. Not only will they have to follow these procedures but they may also have good ideas on how to improve them. Involving your team at an early stage not only gets their ideas but also gets their buy-in to any resulting changes.

The numbers to watch

- Turnover per employee
- Keep a record of how you spend your time for a month. Analyse this to see which tasks can be delegated with staff training or recruitment. Your team can complete the same exercise to see which tasks are worth automating.

Summary

- Once you've grown your business to a certain size you may want to step up or step out (at least a little bit as the 80 hours or so per week is unsustainable).
- Mapping your existing systems is important to maintain consistent standards as you grow.
- Your system maps are also the starting point of your continuous improvement process, either by improving the individual system or by systemising more processes.
- Documenting processes and training your team are the keys to unlocking your own time as you will be able to delegate more.
- Don't be afraid to automate these processes where possible.

Chapter 8

Building and retaining your team

8. Building and retaining your team

If you want to grow your business you will need more resources than a single person, even if you are prepared to put in long hours. If you want a saleable business you will also need to demonstrate that it operates independently of you. Once you've made the decision to grow the business beyond the work of one person, the main decision to make is whether to outsource (and how) or to employ.

Pros of growing beyond a one-person band

- Provides you with income even when you're not working
- Provides some level of cover for your own sickness and holidays
- Allows you access to expertise beyond your own
- Helps you to develop a more saleable business which operates independently of you
- Opportunity to recruit people who are better than you
- Opportunity to delegate the jobs you are not so keen on!
- Reduced interaction with clients or 'on the tools'

Cons of growing beyond a one-person band

- Managing other people may not be your forte
- Managing people takes time
- You may require bigger premises
- Difficulty finding the right people
- What if you take on the wrong person?
- Employment legislation and increased bureaucracy
- Need to run a payroll
- Reduced interaction with clients or technical work

The CEO role

This is the time for honesty and self-evaluation. Are you the best person to be CEO or would you be better suited to another role? Perhaps as chief technical officer or head of sales?

The firefighting skills of a start-up founder are not necessarily those required to run a larger company. Whatever role you take, you will always be the founder. Now may be the time for you to step aside or it may be something to bear in mind for the future.

You don't just want the best team possible but you want the people in the roles they are best suited to.

Issues to consider when recruiting

- What level of knowledge or experience do you require?
- How many hours per week do you require (full time is not compulsory)?
- How will the role change as your business grows?
- Do you need them to work from your premises or will you build a remote team?
- Do you need additional space for them to work? Desk? PC?
- Do you have the communications systems in place for a remote team? Across different time zones?
- What additional software licences or equipment will they need?
- How much time will it take to train them (even a competent, qualified person will need to be trained in your particular methods)?
- How will you cope with the busy interim period while you are trying to train your new starter and do your own work?
- What funding or grants are available for training and other costs?
- Where is the best place to advertise?
- If this is your first employee, will you need a network or will you share IT systems?
- You will need employer's liability insurance.

Finding the right person

I would rather stay small than take on the wrong person. When a key member of staff left and I failed to find a suitable replacement we did have a clear-out of clients.

As a small business owner you want to get the most out of any advert in the local paper. A small box can include your logo, a few job details including salary and a link to your website. This then doubles up as a marketing awareness exercise. The full details of the vacancy can go on your website. Decide what is absolutely necessary for the role and what skills your ideal candidate would hold. These are the things that you won't and will compromise on respectively when sorting CVs and then interviewing. You might want to specify a qualification 'or equivalent experience' to broaden the field.

Leverage your network by letting everybody know what sort of person you are seeking to recruit.

Remember to regularly post the job link on all your social media accounts.

Consider using online job boards – but bear in mind that free or cheap online job boards make it so easy for the candidate to press a button and apply that they are tempted to apply for roles for which they are clearly not suitable. You may receive more applications this way but you will also waste a lot of time filtering through unsuitable CVs. I once advertised for a 'part time, qualified accountant' and was overwhelmed by CVs from part-qualified accountants who hadn't even read the job title.

Advertise for a couple of weeks before printing off all suitable CVs. Note on these CVs whether to interview or reasons for rejection in case of future enquiries. I always emailed rejections and wished them all the best. It's hard for people hanging on wondering when or if they'll hear from you so be kind to everybody you deal with.

I did not use agencies. There may be some good ones out there but there were also some truly poor ones and it was hard to tell the difference until too late. This was learned from my own experience on both sides of the interview table. If you can find a good, reliable agency, they can do a lot of the early work for you.

Work experience

I offered work experience to local schools. While the young ones were there to learn about office life or just because the school was making them do something, I found that sixth formers were more likely to be considering a career in accountancy. They were also able to carry out some useful work and to converse better than younger students when introduced to clients and other business colleagues. This would act as an extended interview if I was thinking of recruiting.

My personal belief is that anyone 'working' much more than a week should get some sort of salary.

If you work with schools then careers fairs and mock interviews are also good ways to identify potential recruits early on.

Subcontractors

Personally I preferred to employ regular workers so that it was clear that they had employment rights and to help them feel that they belonged to the team. When I acquired a small business, there were three subcontractors and one of them chose to come on to the payroll for just these reasons. Employees are entitled to paid holiday and other statutory leave and you will need to pay pensions and National Insurance in addition to their salary, so they are usually paid slightly less than subcontractors.

If you are using subcontractors then you need suitable contracts in place. You also need to be clear on who is responsible for the clients they are liaising with and for prohibiting 'poaching'. (See Chapter 16 for an example from my own experience.) Contracts and job descriptions are important so that everybody is clear on their obligations.

Do be clear about the employment status of any subcontractors. Ensure that you take up references, confirm any qualifications and check that they have professional indemnity insurance. If you are a member of the Federation of Small Businesses (FSB) they have standard contracts for subcontractors as well as a confidentiality agreement. If you are a member of a professional body or trade association they can often help with this too.

Apprentices

My first employee was an apprentice. I had wavered between a part-time qualified accountant who would hit the ground running and a full-time apprentice who I would have to train but who could be trained in exactly the way I wanted things done. The deciding factor was having somebody around to answer the phone when I was out. It worked very well because my apprentice was on day release during term time but in the office for the full five days when I wanted more time with my kids.

Taking on an apprentice allowed me to pay a lower salary, which was the only way that I could afford to grow my business. It also meant that I could afford to set aside 12 months' salary in my deposit account to ensure that I would have enough to at least send him through one year of Association of Accounting Technicians (AAT) training. Beware: under the apprentice scheme there was plenty of paperwork and, with subsequent apprentices, this has increased threefold. For the first apprentice the college came and helped me with the paperwork to enrol him on the course and to help with funding. The course was only partly funded (as he was over 18) so I had to pay the rest but there was also a one-off grant which I put towards a desk, chair, laptop and software licences.

Accountancy training has traditionally followed a mixture of theory and in-house training so the apprenticeship scheme is ideally suited to accountancy trainees. AAT courses are widely available and the college may even be able to help you with recruitment. Many practical jobs have a similar apprenticeship route and it is great to have an expert teaching your newbie the basics which they can then put into practice on site, under your supervision. Make sure that they log on-the-job practical training too.

Induction

A proper induction procedure will help your new recruits to hit the ground running on day one. Taking them out for lunch on their first day will help the team to get to know each other better and help your new recruit feel extra welcome.

Useful items for your induction checklist are:

- Add them to the tea/coffee list with their personalised mug (priorities!)
- Toilet facilities, entry badges, door codes and so on
- Employment contract, and any other formalities such as a confidentiality contract
- Payroll details – P45/6, proof of ID, next of kin, bank details
- Desk, chair, PC and stationery (or whatever their basic tools are) – all ready beforehand
- PC and software logins (make sure that these are set up before the start date)
- Admin procedures – for example, telephones, post in/out, filing of paper and online, expenses, visitors and client visits
- Health and safety training
- Operational procedures or where these can be found if they're not all necessary from day one
- HR procedures – for example, holiday, sickness
- Discuss one-page plan and team KPIs as well as how these relate to any personal or team bonus scheme
- Basic software or other essential training – often online these days

This may seem like overkill for your first employee but the aim is to speed up the time it takes them to settle in and become a net contributor to the team.

I once took over a new job while the previous incumbent continued to use the office and company car while working his notice. I have never felt less welcomed than squatting on the corner of somebody else's desk and sharing their computer for three months and trying to find private space for one-to-one meetings with my new team.

Contracts

You must provide your employees with a contract. If you are a member of the FSB or Institute of Directors (IOD) you will have access to all sorts of contracts to use in-house free of charge. As these contracts are constantly updated do ensure that you are using the latest version for new recruits. It may be more appropriate for you to consult an employment solicitor for more senior staff or for anything unusual.

Your trade or professional body may require additional checks. The Institute of Chartered Accountants in England and Wales (ICAEW) website, for example, has a 'fit and proper person' declaration which the team complete each year as well as a separate confidentiality contract.

Our contracts all had a three-month probationary period. If you do find that you have recruited the wrong person then it is least painful all round to acknowledge the mistake sooner rather than later. Dismissing somebody is a horrible thing to do so ensure that you carry it out legally, according to your procedures, document everything and do it as kindly as possible. You are in control of the situation so be clear and be considerate. Just because they're not the right person for your company/job doesn't mean that they are a bad person so treat them with respect. FSB membership includes access to employment law advice but you may wish to consult your own employment solicitor.

Part time/flexible

The beauty of most work these days is that it needn't be confined to specific hours. You may choose to have core hours or to require a minimum number in the office/shop/site at any time but it is also possible to operate many jobs completely remotely. I know a number of businesses where some or all of the team work in different parts of the world.

All our team had specified days/hours based in the office but were free to switch those hours or work from home by prior arrangement. This flexibility worked to our advantage at busy times when staff would hang on to finish a job knowing that they wouldn't lose out as they could take extra holiday at a quieter time to suit themselves.

Any additional hours worked, at evening events for example, were generally compensated by time off in lieu. This is because it is important that people have time for family and outside interests. When this was not possible during a period when I was recruiting then the overtime was paid instead.

If you're not sure how many hours you will require then a zero-hours contract could be the thing for you. These have received bad press where they have obliged the employee to be available for work but, if obligations are reciprocal, they can be much fairer. You have no obligation to provide work but your employee has no obligation to be available, so you may prefer to specify a minimum number of hours. Essentially your employee will have employment rights but any financial aspects will be based on average hours worked.

If your team operate remotely or part time then communication is key. I allocated clients to different team members so they and others could use our CRM to note important matters for everybody to see. Our CRM also held a copy of all email correspondence to/from the client, although this required a certain discipline in changing the email subject line whenever the subject changed in an email chain. Many businesses – such as maintenance or construction – have some sort of app to control practical jobs on site.

I found that offering flexible working gave me access to some high-calibre women whose hours were constrained by young children. They were complemented by semi-retired staff who wanted long weekends but not school holidays. The only downside was that I ended up with a predominantly female team while I would have preferred a more diverse mix. As a small business this was unavoidable, but increased diversity is something that you might aspire to in order to bring fresh ideas and viewpoints into your business.

There is plenty of evidence that diverse businesses are more profitable than those whose ideas come from a single way of thinking. Why restrict your business to one set of ideas when you could have so much input from people with different backgrounds, skills and personalities?

Results-based management

This is becoming more common as enlightened employers specify outcomes instead of hours. If your employee can complete all their work to the required standard within two days, say, then they can spend the rest of the month on a beach somewhere. The difficulty is in setting the right desired results and communications platforms for teams working together. The logic, however, is good as business depends on the outcomes of the team's work and not the number of hours that they sit at a particular desk.

Looking after your team

I am a great believer that if you look after your team they will look after your business. I once heard that it is more important to look after your employees as, with the right team, it is easy to find new customers. Treat your staff as you want them to treat your best clients.

I held annual appraisals in order to have a formal conversation to document plans, ambitions and training requirements for the coming year. These should never be a substitute for good communication throughout the year but serve as an opportunity to ensure that your people's personal ambitions and those of the business are aligned. If people have aspirations beyond what is possible in the business then it is best not to attempt to hold them back but to help them find a role elsewhere which will satisfy their requirements. If the individual is no longer suitable for your growing and changing business then you will need to provide retraining or even help them to move on. Remember that they are human first and business resources second.

Some of our team were focusing on their families or, for other reasons, had no career ambitions. I changed their appraisal forms to read job ambitions rather than career ambitions so that I could give them the support they needed to flourish in their existing role.

If you struggle with appraisals then you will be pleased to hear that these can be outsourced to a specialist such as Smart Support for Business.

Training

For trainees there is a clear training path with external colleges through day release or home study. As far as possible try to have a structure to your internal, on-the-job training. For qualified or experienced staff you will need to arrange continuing professional development (CPD) to keep them up to date with changing legal requirements, modern techniques and new software.

Good sources of post-qualification training may be local colleges, your trade or professional bodies and suppliers. Training can be online or face to face. Online training makes more efficient use of time without the need for travel or separate coffee breaks but face-to-face training gives the opportunity to network and grow your list of professional contacts and collaborators.

Providing good training may enable staff to leave you but, frankly, why would they want to leave if you are treating them well and encouraging their personal aspirations? There may be times when the nature of the business does not allow you to provide opportunities for your best staff at the right moment but, by encouraging your team to follow their own ambitions when they no longer align with yours, you will still have a reputation as a good employer. A growing business will usually have more opportunities for developing staff.

Personality profiles

You may be a natural 'people person' but, for many of us, people are incomprehensible. Treating people as we would like to be treated doesn't always work. One way of understanding them better is to use DISC profiles to provide a little more insight into different personalities and how to treat people as they want to be treated. These, and other types of personality profiles, attempt to broadly categorise people in order to give an idea of how we each work best. I arranged to profile the whole team and shared the reports, including mine, so that we could understand what made each of us 'tick' and how to get the best out of each other. While the science behind these is sometimes contested they provide a useful discussion document.

There are some accountants who also do this for their clients to ensure that they communicate in the best way.

Organisation chart

An organisation chart shows all the roles within your business from the managing director to the receptionist. Michael Gerber, in his *E-Myth* book (see Further resources), suggests that you draw one up from the beginning. Initially you will be doing every job on your organisation chart and your first team member will probably take on the simplest of the technical work, or perhaps the marketing and admin. As your organisation grows, each person will start to have discrete job roles and the organisation will move from a single team to multiple teams. There are various ways that you can evolve your structure:

- By function, product or specialism
- By client, geography or project
- Matrix management, which is a combination of these two. While great in theory it does require the individual to manage potentially conflicting priorities

Outsourcing

An alternative to recruiting is outsourcing. This can be done locally to an individual or offshore.

Pros of outsourcing

- Increased capacity
- Flexible capacity
- You are not directly responsible for staff
- Gives you access to experts as and when you need them

Cons of outsourcing

- Reduced control over quality
- Need for quality checks
- Data protection and other confidentiality considerations
- Works best with clean/simple jobs

Issues to consider

- Do you want to outsource to an individual subcontractor or to a company?
- How many hours per week/month do you require?
- What level of supervision/checking will they need?
- What sort of interim period should you allow while you are each learning how the other works?
- Do you want a UK outsourcer or are you happy with one based overseas (assuming the work can be done remotely)?
- Will you need to share IT systems?
- How will you safeguard confidentiality and data protection?
- Outsourcing works best with simpler jobs so how will you manage your messier ones?

My story

When a member of staff left and I couldn't find a suitable replacement, I took the opportunity to pass on some of the smaller clients who were no longer suited to us. In spite of this we still had more work than our existing team could handle, so I checked that our contracts allowed us to outsource and chose a firm of chartered accountants in Northern Ireland.

This meant that we shared the same standards but, although wages were slightly lower in Northern Ireland, I made no real margin on the work I outsourced. I chose the company as I wanted to keep the work as local as possible, plus they offered more flexibility in the number of sets of accounts that they would handle for us. The process worked very well on the clean accounts but I did not attempt to outsource any messy jobs because of the extended communication chain.

Our contracts with the outsourcing company included confidentiality clauses and I gave the company read-only access to just the information they needed. They used our software remotely and followed our procedures.

I was very happy with the outcome but I did not continue this as, in choosing to keep the work as close to home as possible, there was little margin. I would do it again as a short-term measure when unable to take on the right in-house staff. I would also consider outsourcing overseas to make some sort of margin rather than to mark time while recruiting and training the right person in house.

Self-care

It's not just your team who need looking after. As their leader it is often easy to forget that you need to be in good health, both mentally and physically.

- Take some sort of regular exercise. Running suits me best as it can fit around my varying schedule. Running is the only time when nobody else is demanding a piece of me and some days it is my only 'me time'. As it is a fairly repetitive action it provides good thinking time and allows my thoughts to become clearer so that I can often come up with solutions to problems that have been baffling me for days.
- Eating well is easier said than done on days when you have lots of business meals out or skip meals while rushing from one meeting to another. Useful snacks to carry are bananas, Babybel cheeses, dried fruit and breadsticks. I usually have an emergency cereal bar in my handbag but these are quite sugary.
- Sleeping well should be possible even when running a business. If you work a nightshift because of a deadline do schedule some recovery time. If your mind is racing at bedtime, then keep a pen and pad at your bedside to note thoughts and ideas before settling down to sleep. I often read business books in bed which stimulate ideas at just the wrong time. If you are regularly sleep deprived as a result of business worries, then you need to seek business advice or even consider becoming an employee again.

While staff and clients are dependent on you performing at your best, you have a duty to look after yourself in order to look after them. Do have a look at our 'Balanced 10' webinar to ensure that you are doing this.

Procedures

We've talked about procedures for carrying out work but you may need two additional procedures, perhaps in your employee handbook, for disciplinary issues and complaints.

Both provide a system for handling problems, the first with internal staff and the latter with external customers. It is useful to have thought these through in advance so that you are not caught on the back foot when things go wrong. These are often drawn up by lawyers, primarily to protect the business, but do consider how you would like to be treated if you were on the other side.

Pitfalls to avoid

- If you make a poor recruitment decision, correct it as quickly as you can but ensure that you do this both legally and kindly.
- Do not recruit the wrong person in desperation. It is better to stay little and good, so look at internal efficiencies or your client/product mix instead and clear out the least profitable until you find the right person to continue your growth.
- Communication is key throughout the year and during annual appraisals.
- Do ensure that you follow a proper recruitment process and have all the legals in place in the event of any future problems or misunderstandings.

The numbers to watch

- Staff turnover
- Staff happiness
- Training costs as a percentage of turnover

Summary

- Once you decide to grow beyond a single person you will need to spend some time managing people, so this is not for everyone.
- You will need to find the right person and provide some level of induction.
- You may choose to recruit a trainee and the National Apprenticeship Service can help to finance courses.
- Recruit wisely and look after your team well while staying the right side of all the legalities.
- If you make a mistake then rectify it rather than let your business suffer.
- Consider part-time workers rather than waiting until you have a full-time vacancy.
- You can choose between employment and outsourcing.
- Look after yourself too!

Chapter 9

Moving into premises

9. Moving into premises

Many businesses start from home and may never want or need to move to external premises. Where I live in North Somerset approximately 70 per cent of businesses are based from home. One colleague told me how, for his first client meeting, he put some empty files on top of the piano and moved a phone on to the dining table even though it wasn't connected to anything.

Options to consider:

- Working from home
- Digital nomad/remote team
- Serviced offices
- Your own premises

Working from home

It takes self-discipline to work from home so this is not for everyone, although it may be the only real choice if you have young children and limited childcare. If you can have a dedicated office within the home this will limit interruptions and keep client information confidential. Unless you keep the door locked it does not stop the rest of the family from borrowing your stapler and so on and failing to return it.

If you're working from home the biggest decision is whether you will see clients at home or will you always visit their premises or meet in coffee shops or elsewhere. If you work alone there are risks to seeing people in unknown places or to inviting them into your home. Online meetings are also an option.

We deliberately bought a former post office with space for a professional-looking office at the front. With a large shop window any visitors were clearly visible from the road and a peephole and a step gave me the advantage as to whether I even wanted to admit callers. The door was kept locked as a default.

Ensure that there are no restrictions on the use of the premises. Read your house deeds properly as many new estates do not allow their freeholders to run a business from home. This is to avoid huge volumes of commercial traffic on a residential street. You will also need to consider whether it is appropriate to have any sort of signage. A small plaque is useful to confirm that visitors are in the right place.

As a former post office, some of our home's original signage is still visible, but it was unclear whether the original business use had ever officially become residential. In order to put up a sign, I decided to play it safe and choose between either have planning permission to run a business from our premises or to apply for planning permission to put up an advertising board. I opted for the former.

There are planning regulations on the size and nature of signage. The main sign was put up while our removal van was unloading and my parents also gave me a traditional brass plaque to put outside by the main door, something that I'd dreamed of when I first started training, even if it isn't so relevant these days.

Remember to notify your insurance company that your home is used for business purposes, although there will probably be no increase in costs until you exceed a certain number of visitors/staff per week.

Your local council may also be interested in charging you business rates. I got agreement from the ratings valuation inspector that the front office was mixed use as it also served as the place where I did my home admin and the children did their homework. When the back office was no longer able to double up as a guest room this had to be classed as business premises, but it fell below the small business limit so there was nothing to pay. Do be proactive in sorting out your rates because the small business rate relief cannot be backdated. On the other hand we had lost Principal Private Residence Relief (PPR) on this part of our home so there would potentially be capital gains tax to pay on the eventual sale of the house.

You can claim a proportion of your domestic costs as a business expense. For a sole trader this is a straight apportionment but, as a limited company, the director charges the company rent and then claims the costs against their personal rental income.

If you are desperate to stay working from home you could consider storing your archiving and marketing materials at another location.

Digital nomad/remote team

These days technology allows many of us to work from anywhere in the world. Even shops can operate solely from the Internet by using a fulfilment agency to hold and distribute their stock. Meetings can be held online. Teams can communicate using software such as Slack and workflow software can control jobs. A virtual office facility can handle your paper post from HMRC, Companies House and other legal bodies.

A remote team allows you to recruit the best people from around the world and to give them a better work/life balance.

Difficulties can be:

- Holding meetings across different time zones
- Cultural differences may necessitate some training as new members join the team. Also you may need some patience with reading different communication styles: one nationality may appear abrupt and almost rude while another may seem to take forever to get to the point and possibly seem evasive
- Discipline of making sure that all essential information is written down and stored in a single system
- Communication generally. It is important that teams are properly trained in how to use software such as Slack
- Team building is harder so part of your communication should be team values and you should also try to arrange team meet-ups as frequently as practical
- A central office with a few remote workers can often be the hardest as those working in close proximity may build a closer relationship, which may leave the remote workers feeling isolated

Serviced offices

These are great for one or more people. As an accountant or solicitor you would probably need a private office rather than a shared one because of confidentiality issues. Your rent and telephone/Internet charges will cover all costs including a shared reception so it is easy to budget. You may have refreshments and meeting rooms included or these will be available to hire.

Serviced offices are ideal for a growing business as you only pay for the space that you are using at any particular time and it is usually relatively easy to take on additional space without changing address. It is also a cheap way of testing out markets in new areas without the cost of a permanent office.

Your own premises

I had been looking at premises for some time just to see what I could get for my money. Then I bought a bookkeeping business to tag on to my main accountancy one. The additional staff and subcontractors forced us to move out of my home and I decided to move to offices in a local shopping centre just two miles up the road in the nearest town.

In choosing new premises you need to consider:

- Do you need a shop window to display goods?
- Do you just need warehouse space with or without an office? This is relatively cheap

- The size of premises including and excluding any shared facilities such as toilets and kitchens
- Professionals may need a separate meeting room or office for seeing clients
- Having a room large enough to hold events, which will mean that you could run more of them
- Having space for good signage visible from the ground floor
- The total cost including rent, service charges, rates and insurance plus an allowance for utilities. As a rule of thumb the total cost of premises will be about twice the rent
- The location of premises for you and staff to get to and where the last one in or out feels safe alone
- The location of the premises for any customers/clients to find you
- Parking and public transport for staff and customers
- The length of lease and any break clauses
- Whether you, as director, have to guarantee the lease thus negating the value of having a limited liability company
- Whether your business would be better off in a town centre or business/industrial park location. Do you need access for goods vehicles?

If the premises are in need of a great deal of work you could negotiate a rent-free period to offset the cost of some of that work. I appointed one of my team to project manage the building overhaul and the move itself. I managed to get our refurbishment work done before we officially signed the lease thanks to a very amenable landlord's agent. I was taking a risk in getting the work completed before signing the lease but I kept an eye on committed costs as well as the progress of the lease.

It is worth using a solicitor for the lease as they can prove very practical in explaining which clauses you could/should change and which ones the landlord is unlikely to move on and what this would mean to you.

Having third-party premises means that you will have to make more effort to ensure that the premises are manned during normal office hours and possibly make additional arrangements for lone working. We installed a magnetic door lock that could be operated via a handset upstairs and a separate lock on our own office door as other residents shared our toilet facilities. There were a few other users who were given the code for the downstairs door by the landlord.

How to find premises

Tell everybody that you are looking, how much space you need and where. Contact local commercial agents and, if you only want a small office, it may be worth contacting your local residential agents too. There is no single website for commercial property and even the agents' own websites have little information.

The simplest way to find property or agents is to drive around the area you are hoping to move to as agents will usually post boards outside vacant premises. Once you get in touch they may well have other sites available.

Signage

Signage is useful in publicising where you are to prospects and first-time visitors. In order to make the most of the footfall in the shopping centre where we had our new offices, we had the traditional shopfront sign over the ground floor entrance plus a more informative sign/ad on a transparency in the window. The most important sign was a 'wayfinder' that stuck out from the building for people to see from further away. Remember that people are unlikely to be looking directly at your office but will be looking along the road. As our offices had a shared staircase I made a cheeky request to put a modern three-dimensional sign on the landing outside our upstairs door and this was granted. It is always worth asking for what you want, politely.

Moving list

Things to arrange when moving offices:

- Rent and service charges
- Rates. You have a limited time period to backdate small business rates relief (SBR). This is available on offices below a certain size but only on one office
- Utilities
- Phone and broadband
- Moving servers unless you are cloud based or have a hosted desktop
- Removals (it is worth getting more than one person along with their van)
- Additional furniture required (there are some good second-hand office furniture stores)
- IT infrastructure – cabling or Wi-Fi for staff plus guest Wi-Fi
- Signage
- Introducing yourself to neighbours and warning them of the extent of any temporary disruption while you move in

- Change of address notifications to clients, contacts and HMRC by email and letter if possible
- Change of address on all marketing material including your website and various online directories
- Change of address on letter templates, email footers and so on
- Mail forwarding
- Buildings and contents insurance
- New risk assessments for health and safety
- Building work and decoration if required
- Refreshments during relocation (and perhaps a bottle of champagne to christen your new home)
- Office-warming party for clients and contacts
- TV licence and PRS for Music licences for streaming TV and/or playing music in the office
- Press release about your new premises
- Delegating the project management of the move to a competent member of the team if possible

The numbers to watch

- Total premises costs per square metre
- Number of square metres per employee (for office space)
- Number of visitors (especially if you run retail or restaurant premises)

Summary

Things to consider when choosing premises:

- Remote working
- How quickly your team is growing and the flexibility of the premises
- Location and accessibility
- Benefits of signage

Chapter 10

Marketing your business

10. Marketing your business

As your business has grown your ideal client has probably evolved too.

Client avatar

Now is a good time to review your client avatar. This is the description of your ideal client. Consider whether these have changed:

- What is their business?
- How big is their business?
- How long have they been going?
- How many staff do they have? Do they have premises?
- Is the owner male or female?
- How old are they?
- Do they have children?
- How do they spend their leisure time?

Try to create a single individual, perhaps even giving them a name, who can be the notional recipient of all your marketing activity.

At the point I sold my first business we were only taking on clients who were serious about their business, and had been around for a few years. They still had to be nice people and we ruled out anyone under the VAT limit, where I didn't think that our advice services were cost effective, as well as most start-ups unless they had high-growth plans and would take on a full advice package. I even put our starting prices on our website to reduce the number of unsuitable enquiries.

When I wrote my first book I had two characters in mind and I'm sure that this is part of why people find it so easy to read. This book also has an intended reader; if you find it useful and enjoyable then that reader is probably you.

Making the most of marketing

'Half the money I spend on advertising is wasted; the trouble is I don't know which half.' – John Wanamaker

The key to getting the most out of your marketing money is to have a good strategy. I initially devised mine from the ideas and other marketing resources of 2020 Innovation (who specialise in accountants) until I discovered *Watertight Marketing* by Bryony Thomas (see Further resources). This book clarified a true marketing process for me.

This is a very obvious area to call in the experts.

A good strategic marketer will help you look at your overall business plan, what products/services you sell and what type of customers you want to attract. They will then help you to put together your marketing plan using the different types of marketing to reach your ideal client.

Branding experts will help you to establish your brand. For some this only means your logo but others will go right into the DNA of your organisation to help you find what you stand for in order to best share that with your public.

Graphic designers look after the visual side of your business with logos and fonts. At Hudson Accountants my first 'logo' was a Times New Roman 'H' designed by yours truly. When I started working with a professional we moved to a sprouting bean in three colours and the strapline 'bean growers, not just bean counters'.

Website designers can come from a marketing or IT background so it is really worth checking out examples of their sites first to see if these fit with what you want/need. If you work with an agency they will have a team that includes visual design, copywriting and technical skills.

Content writers can handle the words for your blogs, adverts, newsletters and website. You may even be able to subscribe to content packages for your industry. I found it best to use a mixture of a standard package for technical content and lots of my own, which I was able to personalise to my ideal client. This is the benefit of an individual copywriter over a standard subscription. Having somebody else write the copy helps to ensure that your blog and newsletters are refreshed on a regular basis.

Some events organisers can also help with the promotion of your events. It is worth checking these out with caution and asking to attend an event that they have organised. Some are good administrators who can get things done but others have more creative flair. You probably need an individual or a company with a mixture of both.

PR companies can help to get your business story in front of people. I have been told that journalists take the news and write the story, whereas content writers have to find your story and make it newsworthy. A good PR article is much more than content as you need an expert with the right connections to get it into the press publications which are relevant to you. As an accountant I only actively promoted in Bristol and North Somerset as most people liked (not needed) to be within 10 miles of their accountant so we targeted local publications. When a local football club was in dispute with their council landlords, my business funded a PR campaign for them which raised awareness nationally, including being carried in a national daily paper. During this highly public period the landlords found some missing paperwork which secured the future of the club. Good PR can make things happen.

There are all sorts of other marketing experts and, while it is unlikely that one individual can provide all these services, it is common for marketers to cross-refer to people they trust and are used to working with.

Marketing agencies are multi-skilled and can provide a more holistic service for a price. It may be worth working with an agency if you have large growth plans and suitable finance.

Types of marketing

There are two main types of marketing: push, where you approach the prospects directly, and pull, where you do things to attract clients. While you need a mixture of both, I believe that good pull marketing attracts better clients and commands higher fees. It will also depend on the nature and value of your products/services.

Examples of push marketing where you actively approach prospects are:

- Advertising
- Sponsorship
- Mailshots
- E-shots
- Telephone calls

Examples of pull marketing are:

- Speaking and writing to demonstrate your expertise as the equivalent of a shop window
- Networking (both online and offline)
- Signage
- A website
- PR

Marketing is often likened to dating, with the process moving from initial awareness to marriage.

It is hard to measure return on marketing as people will usually only tell you the final thing which influenced their decision to contact you, but there is definitely an element of just being around and known for long enough for people to approach you. It is very rarely 'love at first sight'.

I found that a good mailshot would generate 2 per cent leads immediately but of low-level, bread-and-butter clients.

Our signage and my articles in local publications generated a high number of enquiries but only about half of them were good quality. If you are well known people will come to you because they know you. One of our filters when deciding whether a prospect was right for us was to weed out enquiries which started with 'How much?' as I found that these people were too focused on price rather than value. Another filter was to ask why they were looking at changing their accountant and I was always wary of those who wished to leave other reputable accountants. Just because these enquiries were not suitable for us didn't mean that we couldn't help and we tried to refer them to other local accountants. This helped the client and also generated an element of goodwill.

Networking is a very slow process and takes about 6–12 months to generate leads, although I have been fortunate to pick up a good client the first time I visited a new networking group.

Speaking/hosting events is the best opportunity to demonstrate exactly what you are about. This is the closest thing that professionals have to a shop window and has been the source of our best clients but it takes around three years from initial contact to bring them on board.

PR is more effective if you use an expert. Do be aware that you cannot control what is actually written in the press. When I sold my business, one of the local publications used a headline that the Nailsea office was to close, despite the press release making clear that the buyer would retain both offices. Fortunately I spotted the online version and got this corrected. On the other hand another publication used the headline 'Hundreds [of businesses] to benefit' based on the same press release because the editor had picked up on the many clients involved.

Depending on the type of business that you wish to have, I would recommend some quick wins like mailshots alongside some longer-term networking. Once you have enough contacts you can invite then you can begin to develop your own speaking/hosting events. If you have any skill with words then writing articles that provide value to your prospects is easy to fit around most businesses.

Steady state marketing

It is important that you do some marketing throughout the year. If you are too busy with the current set of leads to generate the next set then there will be no next set.

The way to do this is to have a marketing plan. You can generate content during quiet periods which can be drip-fed through busier times or even delegated to a marketing assistant. If you receive too many leads when you are busy this may be an indication that you could increase your prices.

If you attend a networking event but are too busy to follow up immediately then please at least get an appointment in your diary even if it is a while off.

Customer relationship management

A good CRM system is vital to your marketing.

Add on all new contacts who have consented to marketing with a note about how you met them. Update this each time you have another contact with them so that you can see what has the most impact. Adding a little background information is also useful. If you have a poor memory then names of children, favourite football teams and so on are helpful, and if you know how they take their tea or coffee then this can demonstrate that you are interested in them.

Existing clients

Don't forget about your existing clients. These deserve your highest standards of TLC so that they stay with you and are willing to refer new clients to you.

If you have a note of birthdays for other purposes it is a nice gesture to send a handwritten card. If you are running a restaurant then a discount voucher for the month could encourage them to bring their celebrations to you.

New clients

There is a particular welcome window for new clients. Sometimes it can be a single transaction or it may be much longer. I think that accountancy has one of the longest welcome windows of the professions. This is the period of time it takes for clients to begin to feel loyal. This is the period during which clients need their main hand-holding. This is your opportunity to 'wow', to ensure that customers have everything they need to leave your shop full of joy, to ensure that they can use your software, etc. Car dealers and estate agents often include a little gift on delivery/completion. Work out your welcome window and put some extra checks in place to help them to get the most from your product/service during this period.

Many clients complain that accountants and solicitors do not keep them informed of progress. This is probably because we are, ourselves, fully aware of the timescales of carrying out certain work and dealing with the relevant authorities. It is therefore helpful to give new clients an idea of timescales and a contact name for who will be carrying out the work. A client buying a house doesn't need to talk to their solicitor for updates but there could be weekly emails or a particular client manager they can call to track what is happening with their new home.

Builders and other tradesmen are notorious for not attending appointments, getting out the promised quotes or tidying up after themselves. This makes it easy to differentiate yourselves and we have probably spent £100,000 over the years with the firm of builders who did these basics well (and the house hasn't fallen down yet!). Not to mention the referrals that we have given.

Client of the month

A client of the month competition is a good way to thank your favourite clients, give them a bit of publicity, demonstrate good client behaviour to other clients and generate marketing testimonials. The team chose from those who were best aligned with our client avatar and therefore easiest to deal with. We sent them a handwritten thank you card along with some cakes (branded, of course) as well as promoting their business in our monthly e-news. We took the opportunity to say why they were good clients, for example responding to queries promptly, in order to encourage this in others. We also asked them for a quote about how they found our services, which we could use in our e-news and other marketing literature.

Other sources for help:

- Watertight Marketing. Start with buying the book and register this on their website for free updates in order to understand the basics and decide your strategy. Their Webschool has numerous resources that will help you further but is best carried out with a marketing administrator or similar if you do not have the time to do this yourself. I found this an excellent methodology for identifying and setting up the systems required to improve all steps of the considered, thoughtful path to becoming a client of a professional service firm but it will work with any business where the buying decision involves thought rather than impulse or necessity.
- A specialist marketer in your area. They will provide plenty of ideas and material and can even carry out some of the work for you.

The numbers to watch

- Return on investment (ROI): how many new clients and the value of their business compared with the cost of the campaign
- Mailshot responses
- Social media statistics
- Size of mailing list
- Open rates of e-newsletters
- Number of events hosted and number of attendees
- Number of events attended and number of leads

Summary

- Review the ideal client for your scale-up plans.
- Find out where these ideal clients hang out.
- Introduce yourself to them via the appropriate marketing channel.

Chapter 11

Basic bookkeeping

11. Basic bookkeeping

If you're scaling up then you've probably already got somebody doing this for you but if you're still using a manual system then here are some examples of how modern accounting software can really help you to minimise the admin and collect cash faster in your small business.

Why should you pay for software when you can do things on a spreadsheet?

If you use proper accounting software it'll guide you through the bookkeeping process. I'll be honest, it's not as simple as some of the software providers would have you believe, but you can probably manage 80 per cent of the data input and leave it to your accountant to complete the more complex work.

With cloud-based software your accountant can log in to do this work in a way that they can't with a spreadsheet.

After that you can automate more of your business processes by adding apps which integrate directly with your accounting software. I've suggested some apps here but there are hundreds for you to discuss with your accountant to make your business run as efficiently as possible.

Cloud accounting software

I recommend cloud accounting software because it can be accessed simultaneously and securely by you as the business owner, your bookkeeper entering data and your accountant, who can answer all the tricky questions and turn that data into useful information.

You're able to talk to your accountant through the software and have more regular contact with them, which means that they can hopefully suggest some useful things if they're not automatically a proactive accountant. If they are more reactive then you can still ask them to log in if you have any questions.

All three of the software platforms that I've mentioned below will provide you with some basic management information. However, unless you put additional information in, they won't provide you with full management accounts. Please be clear on that. You need to put full information in to get full information out; however, for a small, simple business there may be some reasonably useful information.

Your year-end accounts are easier to prepare if you've got good clear information and this is why I think there is a big trade-off between you doing the data entry versus getting a bookkeeper to do the data entry plus a bit more. If you make mistakes, yes your accountant can sort them out, but it's a darn sight cheaper if you get it right first time and don't overstep your knowledge. Work with your accountant, agree who's going to do what and then stick to your bit of it really well so that the experts can work on their side.

Which software?

The main cloud contenders in my opinion are Xero and QBO, which have very similar functionality these days. This competition means that they are each spurring the other on to provide better software for business owners.

There's also FreeAgent which has less functionality but I find is a good fit for small consultants. Talk to your accountant about which is most suitable for your business but make sure that you are happy with the ease of data input and the useful information that you can extract easily.

Some accountants offer telephone support themselves but all three of the software companies that I mentioned have support included in their package. For technical support on how to use the software I would contact them straight away. The reason you might contact your accountant is if you're not sure what type of expense something is, for instance.

As well as support, all three apps provide online videos and narrative to train you to get the most out of your software. Just Google for any of the terms below to find helpful videos and guidance online. Your accountant may also run training workshops.

Bank feeds

All three companies have the facility to link your bank to your accounting software; then you have the option to pull in the bank statement and just press a few buttons to pull all your bank transactions in.

If you have a bank account that doesn't have a bank feed you can go to your online banking and download a CSV (or other format) file of the statement or transactions. Videos will show you how you can then upload a statement in a semi-manual fashion. Once you have uploaded the statement it will all link through and look almost the same as if you had the direct bank feed.

If you don't have Internet banking then I would seriously suggest that you look for a new bank. It is the 21st century and you have a business to grow. Challenger banks such as Starling and Tide are disrupting the banking sector in spite of being subject to the same Financial Conduct Authority controls and guarantees.

Bank reconciliation

Once you have pulled in all the statement information you have to get it transferred into the core of the software. It's a bit like having a paper statement on one side and entering into your old-fashioned manual ledger from the other side. This is really easy as it uses a combination of bank rules that you set, and machine learning.

The software can suggest a purchase invoice which matches a payment amount or a sales invoice that is the same value as a receipt. This is really my favourite, favourite bit of accounting software. I know, I'm a geek but I just love technology that makes my life easier and makes running my business more efficient.

You may want to save time by asking your accountant or bookkeeper to set up some bank rules for all those recurring transactions such as your rates, bank charges, salaries and other regular transactions.

There are also all sorts of simple data entry apps. Most of these apps work with both Xero and QBO but not always with FreeAgent.

Entering sales quotes and invoices

You can connect your accounting software to your till using Clover, or to your online shop using Shopify. You can have the software available on your phone, so if your team work on site any of you can raise invoices before leaving the site.

If you need to provide a quote then you can do this from your software and just press a button to turn it into an invoice.

You can produce sale quotes from an app on your phone while you are out and about. Email the quote to your customer so they can accept it then and there and you can get on with the job. If it's a bigger job and you want to raise the quote from your office, then you can do that instead. You can see your lists of quotes, which have been accepted, rejected and expired. Your customer can accept the quote online or, if they haven't got back to you one way or another, you can give them a ring and get a verbal acceptance. You can attach all sorts of things to the quote such as drawings and detailed specifications.

Once you've agreed your sales quote you're ready to look at sales invoices. If you've done a quote and it's been accepted as it stands, you can just press a button and turn it into a sales invoice: the first part in the process of getting paid is to raise the invoices. If you're out on site and you finish the job, you can raise the invoice there and then using any of this software.

Repeat invoices

If you are selling something on a contract which is invoiced monthly then you can set up a repeating invoice that goes out every month. I would use this for something like my Growing by Numbers online business course or you might use it for an IT maintenance contract or other subscriptions or retainers.

You can customise your sales invoices and put your own logo on. Don't forget to put your bank details on, as you'll get your cash in faster if you provide all the information your clients need to pay as well as the terms. Your payment terms can go on your quote as well.

Getting paid

You can link up your software to something like iZettle or Square for taking card payments with a PIN, or Stripe or GoCardless for online card payments. With GoCardless you can also set up direct debits, so that you are able to process ongoing payments as well. So there are all sorts of ways of getting paid, but the first bit of it is to issue your sales invoices straight away.

The next step, if you're not paid by one of the instant mechanisms, is to set up the automatic invoice chasing. You can set it up and tweak the email so that it will send out a chasing email every seven days. I suggest you make it fairly polite – you don't need to be too pushy at this stage.

Software won't do the whole of your credit control for you, and you may well still need to pick up a phone, but it will do that first reminder to the people who have just forgotten to pay, or the people who haven't received the invoice.

There is an app that will link to Xero and QBO called Chaser.io that also chases by a series of emails. Chaser has much more functionality than the invoice chaser that's included in the core software and it depends on the nature of your business and clientele if it's worth paying the extra.

Entering purchase invoices and bills

Optical character recognition (OCR) means that you can easily get the information into the software either directly or using an app. There is an expenses module within the main software and there are all sorts of OCR apps that you can add on. Receipt Bank, Hubdoc, Auto Entry and Expensify are the four main ones but there are plenty out there.

You can forward a PDF invoice to a special email account at the application and it will 'magically' appear in your software, or you can take photographs on your phone and submit them via the app. Some of them have a fetch facility where they can access those irritating little online bills which require a login rather than a simple email attachment. This fetch functionality works for a lot of phone bills and utilities.

Stock/inventory

Inventory as the Americans call it, or stock as it is known in the UK, can be handled through the core software for simple processes. Again, if stock is a big part of your business and you want reordering and perhaps individual traceability, then you might want to look at an add-on such as DEAR.

Payroll

This is a complex area of legislation so I would suggest that, unless you know what you're doing, you should ask your bookkeeper or accountant to do this bit for you.

Reports

Now you've got all your information in it's time to see what useful information you can get out. At this stage these are not full management accounts as that requires a little more tweaking by your bookkeeper or accountant, but they should give you enough information to have a little idea of what's going on when you're running your business.

There are five main reports that you might use:

- Profit and loss account (may require accountant input) – shows you how well you're doing over any period of time. I'd recommend that you look at this each month.
- Balance sheet (may require accountant input) – shows what you own and owe at any point in time.
- Aged debtors/receivables report – a list of people who still owe you money.
- Aged creditors/payables report – where you can see all the bills you need to pay. As a small business it might just be that you pay them all as they come in, or you might wait until the end of the week then print off this report to pay them.
- VAT return. There are two parts to the VAT report. The first is the VAT return itself which is submitted to HMRC. The second is all the detailed transactions behind it, so if you have a VAT enquiry you have all the information ready.

Most accounting software will generate these at the push of a button once the bookkeeping is up to date. If you don't have up-to-date books then your reports will be meaningless.

You will also have a dashboard of some key numbers when you first log in.

Accounting software today

Modern accounting software has now become the hub of your business wheel. As you grow, you'll have a full board with separate functions feeding in. Around the boardroom table you might have:

- The CEO (probably you)
- Finance director (perhaps your accountant for now)
- Sales director with their sales software tracking leads through to order fulfilment
- Logistics director with their software to handle stock and delivery routing
- Operations director with staff scheduling software or project management

Just as each director will talk to each other around the table, their software can communicate too. It's quite handy when the numbers are flowing seamlessly so that everybody can see the bits relevant to their area of the business.

Add-ons and apps

There are 800+ official add-ons to the core accounting software and many more that will link using Zapier or Workato rather than the main API, so I'm just going to mention a few of them.

- Stripe is a good one for taking payments by card or manually.
- Clover is effectively a till and a stock control system for shops.
- Shopify is very good for running online shops so you could use it to control the back end of the website sales.
- iZettle is a card machine and it takes a little percentage of all your transactions.
- GoCardless can either take card details online, or use direct debit.
- Receipt Bank I've mentioned, alongside AutoEntry, HubDock and Expensify: OCR software to get your purchase invoices into your accounting software with minimum human intervention.
- Chaser provides a way to chase all your sales invoice payments that aren't collected at the point of sale.
- If you're running projects you might want to look at Harvest and Workflow Max.
- If you want a bit more stock functionality than Xero offers, then look at DEAR.
- For reporting and forecasting try Spotlight or Futrli.

- For shorter range, more accurate cash flow forecasting then look into Fluidly and Float.

There are all sorts of other systems out there as well. If you're not sure then talk to your software company, an app integrator or your accountant.

Mobile

The other beauty of this software is that it's available on mobile so you can have the key functionality in your pocket to handle quotes and invoices and take payment on site. A lot of the OCR apps have an app for your phone as well so you can just take a photograph to upload a receipt instead of losing it in your wallet or allowing it to fade on the dashboard of your van.

Benefits of modern accounting software:

- Ease of use
- Online training
- Free support
- Remote access for your whole team, bookkeeper and accountant
- Links with other business apps
- Key functionality is available on your phone

The numbers to watch

- How much you could earn doing what you are best at compared with handing the bookkeeping over to a competent bookkeeper who will be faster and better than an untrained individual.
- Before investing in any software look at the alternatives and measure the time they will save and other benefits compared with your current method.

Summary

- By now you should be delegating or outsourcing your bookkeeping.
- Modern accounting software is easy to use but can be used better and faster by a qualified bookkeeper or accountant.
- For maximum efficiency link your financial software to other suitable apps.
- Take advantage of the mobile functionality for staff working on site.

Chapter 12

The language of accounts

12. The language of accounts

This chapter is just to give you an overview to help you understand your accounts and the numbers that are useful to you.

Like every profession, accountants use their own jargon between themselves to shortcut explanations. If there is anything that you don't understand then you should ask them to explain. To some extent the language of accounts is used in the wider language of business so it is worth knowing some key words.

Revenue vs capital

Revenue items are things that come in and out of the business, usually within less than a year. This includes things that you sell and the cost of those things that you're selling, be that a physical item or a salary associated with the people providing services that you sell.

Capital items are held in the business for a longer period and they are often used in order to generate revenue, such as a big bit of production machinery, or maybe a company car or van.

If you've got, say, a van in the business and you expect to keep it for three years, then you want to share the cost of the van over those three years. There is a name for this: depreciation.

Depreciation is a notional measure of the wearing out of the van and there are various methods for calculating it. Let your accountant calculate this and don't worry about the detail. Just be aware that, when we talk about depreciation, this is what it is; it's a way of sharing the cost of that van over its useful life.

HMRC have their own version of depreciation called capital allowances. Again, let your accountant do the calculations. This is one of the reasons that your accounting profit (as shown in your accounts) is not the same as your taxable profit (as shown on your tax return).

Prudence

Prudence is one of the fundamental things that we need to consider when preparing accounts. It is why accountants are often seen as cautious. But it's not really the accountants who are a cautious lot, it's what investors like to see.

We have to be prudent, so that usually means that if somebody has verbally agreed to buy something, you don't recognise that sale until it has actually been delivered. Income is recognised only when it is certain.

On the other hand, if there was something that might be a bit of a cost, depending on the likelihood, you will record the cost when it's probable that it's going to happen. For instance, if you think that somebody is not going to pay you, then you would record it as a bad or doubtful debt.

Income only goes into your accounts when it's earned but the costs may go in as soon as you are aware that they will probably be incurred. Again there are detailed rules that your accountant will follow.

As you can imagine there can sometimes be a grey area concerning when something should be reflected in the accounts. HMRC rules on provisions for doubtful debts are not the same as those for preparing accounts. In addition to these rules, point of sale/commitment on certain costs can be unclear. At what point does legal ownership of the item transfer? And does this vary according to the commercial substance of the transaction?

Materiality

If you're generating £1m turnover, then what sort of difference in the cost is going to change any decisions that you might make? At what level will it cause investors or people reading the accounts to form a different opinion? This is known as materiality.

So if it's plus or minus £1 then it doesn't matter on a £1m turnover. It probably doesn't even matter on a £100,000 turnover.

When you give your books and records to your accountant, they will be preparing accounts that are correct, which represent the true situation in your business. But they might not be 100% accurate because of various reasons. They won't be looking to make sure that everything is in exactly the right place. As long as it fits within that concept of materiality they will be happy. Both HMRC and your auditors (required for medium-sized companies and some others) will have their own acceptable level of materiality.

This gives you two main sets of numbers in your financial statements (accounts).

Profit and loss account

You have a profit and loss account which is usually over a 12-month period. This shows you the flows into and out of your company during the year. When you have management accounts you can choose to look at the last month, or quarter or any duration that you like.

Balance sheet

The balance sheet is like a photograph. It's a snapshot at the last day of the accounting period that shows how all your assets and liabilities are held.

Assets

Assets are the things you own, such as a van, or a stock of items that you've bought but not managed to sell yet. They might be the people who owe you money, or the cash in your bank. These are the things which you own or are entitled to.

Liabilities and debts

Liabilities are the money that you owe to others. They are things like the trade creditors/suppliers that you bought things from, but haven't quite paid the bills yet. They could be things called accruals which are bills that you haven't received yet, but you've committed to and you know they're coming. So for instance your electricity is paid in arrears. You can see that you've used a certain amount of electricity today and you will expect the bill to come in. That's an accrual.

There might be other bits of money that you owe in loans. You'll owe some sort of corporation tax if you've made a profit. You may owe some PAYE for your staff and VAT as well.

At the very bottom of the balance sheet (in the UK) is what the shareholders are entitled to. That includes their shares at face value. If you've got 100 shares in your company at £1 each, that is £100 worth of share capital. It's also the various reserves, but mainly the profits from last year that weren't dished out by way of tax and dividends.

This is not a book about the detailed accounting rules and complexities but you need some basics to understand why your accountant does certain things with the numbers. If you still have questions after reading this then ask your accountant. I'm sure they will be very happy to answer them for you but there is no need for you to have more than an overall understanding.

Matching income and expenditure

And then there is the concept of matching income and expenditure. Consider the sales that have been made in this period, irrespective of whether they've been paid or not. You might just work on a cash basis (cash, confusingly, refers to any immediate payments such as cash or cards – it excludes trade creditors). It's fine for micro companies (under £1m turnover) to do cash accounting but once you reach a certain size, then you will need to do accruals accounting and you will have to match your income and your committed costs for the period.

Debtors/receivables

'Debtors' refers to sales that you've made that haven't yet been paid for. You'll never see debtors on a cash accounting basis, but they are part of the accruals basis. It's those sales invoices that are still waiting to be paid at year end.

If you are one of those lucky businesses, such as a shop or restaurant, that gets paid at the point of sale then you won't have any trade debtors. If you are an architect, for example, you would do the work, raise the invoice and then wait to be paid. This means that you are likely to have debtors who owe you money.

If you are running a plumbing business, you could do either. If you're working for a big construction firm or a building project, you do the work, raise the invoice and wait to be paid. But if you go into somebody's home and fix their burst pipe or their broken boiler, that's a different thing and you could expect to be paid there and then on site (there's some simple bookkeeping automation that allows you to take that payment via your phone).

Cash is vital for a small business owner but debtors are the next best thing as they represent cash that is due to you.

Creditors/payables

Creditors are the flip side of debtors – they are the people you owe money to. For instance, your accountant may send you a bill and you will pay it (promptly I hope). Many accountants these days are putting things on standing order or direct debit to save their clients the admin associated with making payments. The amount you owe your accountant is a creditor item until it is paid.

If you've bought building or plumbing supplies at somewhere like Travis Perkins they will give you the invoice at the time of sale but you won't need to pay until the end of next month, or whatever payment terms you have agreed. The same thing applies with PAYE, VAT and corporation tax owed to HMRC.

Prepayments

Prepayments are a special kind of debtor item. They are things that you have paid for in advance. For instance, let's say I'm going to a conference in a few months' time: I've paid for the ticket for the conference, I've also paid for my hotel. But because they haven't happened in this accounting period, they are what we call prepayments; they are paid in advance and they don't relate to this accounting period.

Accruals

On the flipside of the prepayments there are accruals. A typical example is your electricity bill, which is paid in arrears. You might know that you pay a couple of hundred pounds a month for electricity but you haven't received the bill yet for this month. Instead you will have an accrual for that £200, or whatever your bill is expected to be.

Debtors, creditors, accruals and prepayments: these are the common differences between accruals and cash accounting, which is based purely on the money in your bank. As a small start-up you may have used cash accounting so when you get your full accounts they might look a bit strange. If anything looks strange or you don't understand it then please ask your accountant to explain it. There are webinars and other resources on our website on the subject of finance for business owners.

Stock

A lot of businesses have stock, some don't. If you've sold £2,000 worth of frisbees and you've bought £1,500 worth it may seem as though you've made £500 worth of profit. But, if you still have £300 worth of frisbees in stock then you've really only sold £1,200 worth of frisbees.

In this case you would show the £300 of frisbees that you still own on your balance sheet. During the period in which you've sold these frisbees, which cost £1,200 and for which you've charged £2,000, that gives a profit of £800.

Profit margin vs mark-up

	£	£
Sales	2,000	3,000
Cost	1,200	1,800
Gross profit (GP)/margin	800	1,200
GP %	800 / 2,000 = 40%	1,200 / 3,000 = 40%
Mark-up	800 / 1,200 = 67%	1,200 / 1,800 = 67%

The £800 profit is sometimes referred to as your profit margin. This may be expressed as a percentage, as in the table above.

The other word you will hear is mark-up, which is how much you increase your cost by to set the selling price. If you are a straightforward retailer it's relatively easy. If you buy something in for £1,200 and you sell it for £2,000, it's a mark-up of £800, or 67 per cent mark-up on the cost. This is commonly used to set prices in-store by adding a pre-agreed mark-up to all costs.

It's important that you know which is which. There is a difference between margin and mark-up. Within your business you will probably use one or the other, but when talking to your accountant, they may use the opposite one. If you're not clear, ask your accountant – you are paying the bill after all. You need to understand your numbers and just ask them if they can remind you about gross profit and mark-up, and which is which. They will be very happy to explain it to you.

Debtor days

This is a measure of how long it takes you to collect the money that people owe you. So if you offer payment terms of seven days from the end of the month in which the invoice is raised, then on average, your debtor days, if everybody pays on time, will be around about 22 days (depending on whether you raised the invoice on day 1 or day 30). That's an average of 15 days in that month and then you add the seven days on at the end. If your terms are seven days but your debtor days are 32, you've got a problem. If your payment terms are 15 days you would want debtor days of 30 (15 + 15). In this case 32 days is probably not a problem. If you offer payment terms of seven days from invoice then your expected payment time would be just 7 days.

Debtors (£)	6,000	3,000
Sales (£)	24,000	24,000
Debtor days	(6,000 / 24,000) * 365 = 91.25	45.625

Stock days and stock turnover

Stock days shows how many days' worth of stock you have in place, and your stock turnover measures how fast your stock moves on to become a sale. You want stock days as low as possible, because you don't want to be paying for stock to sit in your warehouse doing nothing. This is why a lot of the big automotive companies use 'just in time' manufacturing so that stock arrives just as it is needed and not a moment too soon.

If you've got high stock days you need to hold less stock, but then you've got the risk of not being able to service your customers properly. There are always compromises in the real world. And some of that depends on your suppliers. If it takes 30 days to get an order from the supplier, then you need to be ordering 30 days before you need it. Probably 32 or 33 days, just to make sure you've got a bit of flexibility in that.

Stock turnover is how often that stock gets sold in a period. You want your stock turnover to be as fast as possible. Especially if you're selling food or something with expiry dates.

Stock (£)	3,000
Cost of sales (£)	24,000
Stock days	(3,000 / 24,000) * 365 = 45.625
Stock turnover (£/day)	24,000 / 3,000 = 8

The big motor companies have detailed stock management systems and the commercial clout to insist on rapid delivery from their suppliers. When you're choosing suppliers you might consider a different supplier who delivers faster or more reliably, even if that means paying a little bit more, in order to save tying up money in your own stock. Just so you can still make those sales. Because the worst thing is not being able to fulfil a sale.

Trading solvently

As a director your have a legal obligation to ensure that the company is trading solvently. This means that you should be able to meet all your debts as they fall due. There are some simple liquidity ratios to help keep an eye on this.

Liquidity ratios

The quick ratio is sometimes known as the 'acid test'. This looks at the solvency of the business, the numbers in your accounts, asking 'If we need to raise cash quickly, what have we got?' It excludes the stock, but includes the debtors (the people who owe you money). Ring them up and get that money in now. It also includes the cash in your bank. The total debtors + cash is divided by the money that you owe within the next 12 months. (That's trade creditors and the taxman and maybe a few other bits.) Your quick ratio should be at least 1 to be comfortable but it depends on what is normal for your industry.

$$\text{Quick ratio} = \frac{(\text{debtors} + \text{cash})}{\text{creditors}}$$

The current ratio also includes your stock, so that takes a bit longer because you need time to sell the stock, to turn it into debtors, to then turn it into cash divided by the same liabilities and the money that you owe to other people. This should be higher than your quick ratio, because you've got longer to sell and, depending on your industry, that might be 1 or 2.

$$\text{Current ratio} = \frac{(\text{stock} + \text{debtors} + \text{cash})}{\text{creditors}}$$

The exact number it should be depends on the nature of your business. For instance, if you run a food shop where you get paid straight away, then you don't have any debtors, so it's just cash in your quick ratio. In your current ratio, because it's food, you're turning it over very quickly, so it's your stock and your cash. Make sure cash is included. If you need to find out what's about right for your industry then your accountant should be able to tell you that, or any decent advisor should be able to give you an idea of what range is normal.

Stock (£)	5,000
Accounts receivable (£)	6,000
Cash (£)	2,000
Current assets (£)	13,000
Current liabilities (£)	10,000
Current ratio > 1	13,000 / 10,000 = 1.3
Quick ratio/acid test > 1	8,000 / 10,000 = 0.8

Gross vs net profit

Gross profit is the sales minus the specific costs of those sales and is quite straight-forward. If you are selling a particular item, then it's quite clear what the cost of your sales is. You also have overheads like your shop rent and staffing. Your gross profit less all your other overheads is your net profit before tax (PBT).

In construction your sales are a mixture of your labour and the materials that you've used. So you would expect to see the same margin and mark-up on your materials because you will maybe add 10–20% on each time. You will also make money on your labour rate. Your overheads will be things like the running costs of your vans.

Direct costs are those costs directly related to the sale. Overheads are the things that are devoted to running the business, as it were.

Sales - direct costs = gross profit

Gross profit - overheads = net PBT

Fixed vs variable costs

Variable costs are the sort of things whereby the more you sell, the more it costs. Fixed costs are fairly independent and unchanged by the volume of sales. Your accountant's bill will be fixed compared with the volume of sales. Now it might be that as your business grows, there's more to be done on the accountancy side, so it's not entirely fixed and there will be a bit of a step change.

If you have a van, the fixed costs are your rental, road tax and insurance, and your maintenance is fairly fixed each year – it tends to relate more to the age of the vehicle – and your variable costs are the amount of fuel that you put in, which relates to your mileage. If you've got offices, the rent is always fixed. Now it might be that you get bigger offices and therefore you have higher fixed costs, but it's usually fixed for a period.

Opportunity costs

People often don't think about this, but opportunity costs are quite important. If you insist on doing your own bookkeeping, it might appear to be zero cost compared to paying a bookkeeper to do it. But actually, if you're doing an hour of bookkeeping you could be losing out on an hour of your real work. You might be charging £40 or £100 an hour so your opportunity cost is the £40 or £100 an hour which you are losing out on. A bookkeeper might cost £15–£25 an hour so would be a cheaper option than doing it yourself.

You're better off just handing over your bookkeeping to an expert and getting on with what you are really, really good at, because you earn more money doing that. There are lots of jobs that people hang on to themselves because they think it's free, but actually it's not. And it's the same when you come to recruit staff. People might say, 'I'm working 80 hours, because I can't afford anybody else to do it for me.' But actually, staff can be relatively cheap or you can outsource in other ways. So look at the opportunity costs, the opportunities you're missing out on because of the things that you are insisting on doing yourself.

Management accounts

You can have your management accounts in any format you like. You don't just have to have the categories according to your statutory accounts. You can have as many different cost types as you find useful and you might want to vary these over time. If you're focusing on your marketing costs, they might just be lumped together in marketing one year and the next year you might want to separate out the costs of advertising, social media, networking, trade shows and so on. You can split out more detailed information or you can have it grouped together as one.

Because they're *your* accounts, they need to be useful to *you*, to help *you* to manage *your* business. The other thing you can do if you've got different products or sectors is to look at the profitability of each of these separately. You might want to compare business in two different countries.

For instance, I provide coaching to accountants but I also provide coaching to other sorts of businesses. With two main markets I want to know what costs relate to servicing accountants and what costs relate to looking after other businesses. I can have reports for both sides of my business just as I have written books and courses for both.

As you get bigger you might have separate departments and want to see the costs of each department. By using cost centres or tracking codes you can see the costs of salaries, company cars, advertising and maybe a bit of customer entertaining in the sales department – compared with, say, production, which will have a different set of salaries and equipment and things like that. So you can separate out seemingly identical costs like salaries and see how they are helping your company.

It is also possible to look at the profitability of individual projects.

It's not possible to include several textbooks of accounting training in just one chapter but I hope this has helped to explain some of the jargon. Do ask your accountant if there's anything that you're not sure of or there are further resources on my website.

Summary

This is some of the common jargon that a business owner needs to be aware of:

- Capital and revenue
- Prudence
- Materiality
- Profit and loss account
- Balance sheet
- Assets
- Liabilities
- Matching income and outgoings
- Debtors
- Cash = cash + bank + debit and credit card payments

- Creditors
- Prepayments
- Accruals
- Stock
- Gross profit, gross margin and mark-up
- Gross vs net profit
- Fixed vs variable costs
- Opportunity costs

Remember that management accounts are for *your* benefit.

Chapter 13

Writing a business plan

13. Writing a business plan

Your business plan is the map of where you want your business to end up and how you intend to get there. The level of detail that you need will depend on whether the plan is for internal use or to seek external funding. If the latter then it is worth working with your accountant; however, if it is just for your own planning then you may choose to do some or all of it yourself.

Time period

It is normal to prepare a detailed monthly plan for the first 12 months and then annual figures for the next four years. It is unusual to look beyond five years into the future as it becomes less certain and there is more chance of unforeseen changes in your business, industry, legislation, etc.

The numbers

You would usually start with a sales plan:

- What products or services will you sell?
- Are you planning any new products or services?
- Which markets will you sell to? These can be geographical or different industries.
- Will you expand into new markets?
- How much will you charge?
- How big do you want your business to grow?
- What market share do you have now and how much are you aiming for?
- What will your competitors be doing in response to your activities or will you be following a market leader?

Plan how you intend to grow each area of your business. This may require more people and more marketing so consider what you need to do in this area.

Stock

Do you need to purchase items for resale? Or will you buy raw materials to produce your own products? Who will be responsible for purchasing these and negotiating prices? Will you be able to get any bulk discounts? What is the delivery time and how much stock will you need to hold? Where will you store this stock?

The people

Draw up a rough organisation chart as at today and in five years' time. How will you get from your team today to your future team over the next few years?

Consider what skills you will need in each area:

- Sales
- Marketing
- Technology
- HR
- Legal
- Finance
- Distribution and storage
- Manufacturing
- Purchasing
- Quality
- Health and safety
- Environment
- Management

How many people will you need in each department and at what level? This should help you to work out your approximate wage bill. Don't forget to add on employer's National Insurance, pensions and any company cars or other benefits.

People will need to be trained and you will also need adequate staffing to cover for holiday and sickness.

The technology

Will you need additional technology? Will automation help you to scale your business? Will you require in-house experts for this or will you use consultants or software companies?

There will be a cost associated with this.

Marketing

What will you need to spend on people and other marketing resources in order to win the planned sales? Ensure that there is decent customer service throughout the organisation so that you are able to retain your hard-won customers and encourage them to refer you.

Assets used in the business

- What will you need in the way of premises for your people and your business? Will you rent or buy or even build?
- Will you increase the size of your main premises or run a series of branches? Will you even need premises if you run a service business with remote staff?
- Will you need a factory, warehouse, storage yard, shop or offices? What sort of location and quality?
- Will you need company cars or delivery or maintenance vehicles? Will these be leased or purchased outright and will you need finance or to release equity in the company?
- Is there any machinery that you will need? Computers and office furniture?

Legal and professional support

As you scale up you need to ensure that you have all the formalities in place. Do you need any licences? Are your health and safety procedures up to date and monitored? What about planning permission and architects for any property expansion? Do you need to update any of your legal paperwork such as:

- Shareholders' agreement
- Directors' service contracts
- Articles of association
- Terms and conditions of sale
- Employee contracts and handbooks?

Are all your operations manuals complete and up to date?

All of these actions will incur some sort of cost. These should be reflected in the financial section of your plan.

Once you have worked out all the numbers you will be able to see if the business is viable. Now you will start a series of iterations as you tweak costs to see the effect on income. For instance, can you reduce your marketing and still win the same amount of sales? What will be the impact on cost and customer service levels if you outsource all your deliveries to a specialist logistics company or couriers?

Once you are satisfied that the numbers are credible your business plan can now be tidied into the following:

- Objectives
- Market and competitor analysis

- SWOT analysis – this is a simple way to present the **strengths** and **weaknesses** of your business, **opportunities** for growth and improvement and any potential **threats**, along with ideas on how you can avoid or negate them
- Sales plan in numbers and written explanation of actions
- Write-up of your other actions derived from answers to the questions above
- 12-month detailed profit and loss account summarising the impact of the actions in the first year
- Five-year profit and loss account showing the impact of your actions in the longer term
- 12-month and five-year balance sheet and cash flow to ensure adequate resources and funding are available to carry out your plans
- Anything else which is useful to your understanding of your plans and ambitions.

Summary

Essential components of your business plan are:

- Objectives
- Sales
- Marketing
- Staffing
- Other resources/costs
- Assets required
- Cash flow

Chapter 14

Controlling your cash flow

14. Controlling your cash flow

'Turnover is vanity, profit is sanity, cash is king.'

I can't find who originally said that but it is very true.

Lack of cash is the main reason that small businesses fail but many people still don't prioritise their cash flow.

Ways to improve your cash flow:

- Increase income (see Chapter 5, 'Setting your prices')
- Get paid sooner
- Reduce bad debts
- Reduce outgoings (see Chapter 6, 'Budgeting and controlling costs')
- Pay suppliers later

Starting up

When you set up a company you need to pay for certain things, probably immediately as you have no credit rating, or there is a financial penalty for extended payment terms.

Getting paid sooner

Retail is good because customers pay straight away, although there may be a delay in waiting for your chosen card processor to transfer the card payments.

Construction is hard with large amounts of cash tied up in materials and labour. Delays along the way do not just add cost but also delay final payments. There is commonly a retention clause in the contract which means that the final 10 per cent, usually the profit on the deal, may be delayed a further 12 months. Even then you may need to fight to get it which is why it is worth having suitably qualified and experienced solicitors involved from the outset. Experienced negotiators can also help with staged payments.

Accountancy services are also slow. Traditionally, even once you have a client signed up you have to wait for their year end, chase the work in, do the work and then invoice before you will receive any cash.

If service companies can charge fixed fees you and your client will know, in advance, what the annual fee will be. Most small businesses are happy to spread this cost over 12 months rather than face a large bill, even if it is much later. This means that you and they have more predictable cash flow.

With predictable income you can arrange collections by standing orders. These are free but need to be updated by the client for price increases and one-offs. You could also collect by direct debit, which is under your control but has an associated cost. Our usual terms were monthly payments, with half the annual fee paid before the year end, which sometimes meant a larger initial payment if the client came to us after their year end.

An additional benefit is the reduced credit control costs and, as you won't be constantly chasing invoices, a better relationship with clients because there are no surprise bills.

If you are already in business and worried about switching to monthly payments please be reassured that most clients actually prefer to pay this way. If you are still wary then start with new clients only and perhaps a simple circular email offering this method to your existing clients. I estimate that around a third will sign up immediately with a further third signing up when prompted a second or third time. It is then up to you whether you chase the stragglers because your cash flow will have improved just from two-thirds of your clients.

For clients who do not wish to spread the cost you might require the full payment up front, or at least a large deposit, before starting work. If you have costs to pay out such as materials or salaries then it is reasonable to ask for payment on account and staged payments. Be careful to specify these stages in your original contract terms and don't leave them to the client to determine. Take care to avoid such stages as 'approval' of work as this is very vague and it may be that the work is never 'approved'.

Some small trades ask for customers to pay for materials directly at the builders' merchant. This saves the business having to find the cash themselves.

You are not a bank! Your business is not lending money to clients through extended credit terms. Ensure that you get paid as much up front as possible and chase debts as soon as they become overdue.

Football clubs issue season tickets which are paid for in March for a season that doesn't even start until August let alone finish until the following May, so fans are paying 5–14 months before receipt of 'goods'. And these don't even come with a quality guarantee as most dedicated fans will know. If even football clubs with multi-million-pound losses can get their customers/fans paying this far in advance then why can't other businesses?

For those unable to pay for the season up front, our local club has negotiated a season ticket loan facility with a third party. The fan pays the additional cost of this and the club receives the cash immediately. You could refer your clients to similar financiers.

How to minimise bad debts or slow payment

- Remember that a sale is not a sale until it has been paid.
- Check your prospect's credit rating before you try to sell to them. Perhaps they are keen to try a new supplier because they have exhausted their credit facilities elsewhere. If you later find that you've sold to poor credit risks you can end up paying for goods, staff time, software and so on but never receive any payment in return. If you have to wait a long time to receive payment then you need to find a way to pay your own suppliers and your staff salaries in the meantime.
- Make sure that your terms and conditions of sale are clear. These should be specified in your contracts and on your invoice.
- On completion of work you could arrange a courtesy call to check that the client is happy, and that they have received the invoice and approved it for payment. This gives you time to rectify any mistakes or perceived problems with the service.
- If payment is not received on the due date then call straight away. This can be a polite enquiry to ensure that everything is OK. If payment is delayed, can they give you an expected date so that you can negotiate your overdraft? Decide whether to continue working with this client or whether to put them on 'stop' so that the debt doesn't grow further.
- Seven days later, or whenever the payment was promised, chase them again, perhaps with a formal letter. You can then start a series of letters leading to legal action if the debt is still unpaid.
- If you use Xero then some of this chasing can be automated with invoice reminders. Alternatively, Chaser.io connects to both Xero and QBO and provides a more sophisticated reminder system.

Paying your suppliers later

Always pay your suppliers on your agreed terms.

You can negotiate longer payment terms or it is often possible to pay some bills, such as insurance, over 12 months for little or no extra cost.

There is a cost of administration when making payments so it may be simpler to make payments on receipt of invoice or on a fixed day each week or month.

How to obtain finance including overdrafts

Having a business plan and management accounts is key to arranging finance. This is how you can explain your business to the bank (or alternative financier) and how you show that you can afford to pay their interest charges as well as repaying their loan. Not only are the management accounts themselves important as part of obtaining finance, but the fact that they are readily available shows that you are truly in control of your business and understand the financial implications of your business decisions.

Armed with your management accounts and cash flow forecast you should have no problem obtaining finance as banks are still happy to lend in low-risk situations. Banks will lend to support expansion or growth and our clients have received finance for their acquisitions. Banks will not lend to support ongoing losses with no realistic plan for repayment.

You can also look at invoice finance – borrowing against amounts due – as a short-term or ongoing source of cash. There are various ways of assigning your invoices and costs will vary accordingly.

For bigger projects or for start-ups you may need to look beyond banks. Take a look at Capitalisers.com, a service which is accessible via your accountant and gives access to multiple financiers at once. It's a bit like MoneySuperMarket but for business finance. If you don't need the cash immediately then it is often cheaper to agree finance ahead of time.

The numbers to watch

- Cash at bank
- Overdue debtors
- Debtor days
- Stock days
- Creditor days
- Quick ratio

As you can see there are plenty of numbers to watch in this area because cash flow is a potential problem in most businesses. (See Chapter 13.)

Summary

You need cash to pay for many things in your business but you also need cash from the company to pay for many things in your personal life. You need cash to book your holiday, you need it to buy your child's birthday present and you will, eventually, need it to live on in retirement.

In order to do this you will need to:

- get more money in sooner
- only deal with creditworthy clients unless you receive payment in advance
- consider arranging access to finance for clients
- pay less money out and later
- plan your cash flow requirements in plenty of time.

Chapter 15

Calling in the professionals

15. Calling in the professionals

So far we've talked about what needs to be done but not so much about *who* should be doing it. When you first start up a business money is usually tight but you have more time to do things yourself. And it can be fun learning new skills. But at some point you need to call in the professionals, who will do the job cheaper (compared to the opportunity cost of your time), faster and most definitely better.

Accountant

Your accountant has a wealth of expertise acquired over a number of years. A chartered accountant will have three years' postgraduate training and experience. If it is their own business they will have at least two years experience since gaining that qualification. This means that they have around 10,000 hours of expertise. Minimum. Yet many people still try to do their own accounts, with little idea of tax law, which changes every year.

Numerous surveys show that accountants are the most trusted advisors.

Yes, there are some bad apples but here are some ways to avoid them:

- The title 'accountant' can be used by anybody and is not protected in law. Select a chartered or certified accountant who has the letters ACA, FCA, ACCA or FCCA after their name. This means that they have reached a minimum technical standard and Fellows have 10 years' post-qualification experience (and probably the grey hairs to go with it). They may have trained in an accountancy business or as an accountant in a different sort of business. This will give them a slightly different set of skills.
- ACMA and FCMA are chartered management accountants who usually have more expertise in the numbers to help grow your business but less training on the tax side. Ask about their background and experience to decide if this would be more suitable for you. Alternatively you might choose separate accountants to work with you on the tax side and the management reporting.
- CTA is a chartered tax advisor and they are the recognised experts in this field. Some work directly with the public but most provide a source of expertise for accountants. Larger accountancy firms will employ their own tax experts for advice and planning on tricky areas.
- Chartered accountants are regulated by their professional bodies, sign up to a code of ethics, have to stay technically up to date and will have professional indemnity insurance in the event that something does go wrong.

- Many accountants advertise themselves as business advisors but there is no clear definition of this term. Often their skills are in tax advice and access to finance. Others can offer a broader range of advice to actively help you to grow your business. Again, be clear on what you need and what the accountant is offering.

My story

Although I am a Fellow of the Institute of Chartered Accountants (FCA), approximately half my experience has been from working in non-accountancy businesses, where I was responsible, not just for finance, but strategy, IT (including protecting the business and our customers from the millennium bug), quality assurance, fleet management, facilities maintenance and general support services. I also picked up a lot about marketing from a friendly marketing director who was keen to share his expertise with somebody so enthusiastic. This gave me a large breadth of skills myself as well as liaising with experts in all these separate fields.

The other half of my career has been spent in accountancy 'practice', where I have provided a range of accountancy, tax and business advisory services over the years. Working with diverse businesses is helpful for borrowing ideas from one industry and adapting them for a different business. Even when setting up my own accountancy business I focused primarily on bringing in the best modern practices from all industries rather than running a traditional accountancy practice.

Things to think about when choosing your accountant:

- Qualified by experience (QBE) or ex-HMRC: while some of these can provide an excellent service it can be more 'hit and miss' than with a qualified accountant who is a member of a professional association.
- It is important that you find an accountant who is not just technically competent but somebody that you can get along with. Having a good personal relationship and open communications will enable you to get the best out of your money.
- In all but the smallest practices, after the initial meeting, you may not deal with the owner themselves but they will be overseeing all the work. Richard Branson does not install every Virgin Media line. Make

sure that you are happy with your regular contact person as well as the accountant you first spoke to.

- Ask for recommendations from businesses that you aspire to be like. Smaller businesses may be happy to refer you to their mate but, if you are scaling up, you may need a different sort of accountant from those who deal with smaller start-ups. There will be different tax issues to consider as well as different business problems for which you may seek advice.
- Beware of tax schemes which sound too good to be true. You may have heard of numerous cases, including some quite high-profile ones, where people have been caught out by these schemes. Always ask your accountant about the risks as well as the benefits so that you understand what you are signing up to.
- No matter who you engage as your accountant, the ultimate responsibility for your accounts and tax returns lies with the directors. Ask any questions that you need to to satisfy yourself before you sign them off.

Bookkeeper

Most business owners can use modern accounting software to do their own bookkeeping at the start. As you grow you may choose to outsource the data input to free up your time.

Once you have engaged a bookkeeper they can do some of the work which your accountant was previously doing. They should understand the tax and VAT implications of all your transactions (or know which to flag for your accountant). They will be able to reconcile (check that everything balances) in your software and catch any queries early on.

Some bookkeepers can produce year-end accounts and tax returns for simple businesses. These are probably enough for a start-up but, as you start to grow, your business will become more complex and you may need to move to a chartered accountant at this stage.

Needless to say I have numerous tales of the relief that many clients have felt at being able to hand over a task which they hate to a competent but friendly individual who loves nothing more than to create order out of the chaos.

Here are some pointers towards finding a good bookkeeper:

- Some accountants employ bookkeepers, which means that everything is under one roof and, hopefully, the accountant and bookkeeper are talking to each other regularly. Even if they don't employ them directly most accountants know the better bookkeepers around.

- There are a number of recognised qualifications for bookkeepers. The AAT trains accounting technicians, who can do more than just the bookkeeping as they have some tax and accounts training. There are four levels to achieve the full qualification so do ask.
- ICB (Institute of Certified Bookkeepers) members purely study bookkeeping and are required to have less experience than AAT members. That said, all their expertise is in bookkeeping but don't expect any of the extras.
- Like the professional accountancy bodies, AAT and ICB members sign up to a code of ethics, have to stay technically up to date and will have professional indemnity insurance in the event that something does go wrong.

A good bookkeeper is worth their weight in gold!

Business coaches, mentors, consultants and advisors

This is another can of worms as, although there are a number of coaching qualifications, there is no sort of regulation. Unfortunately too many of the coaches and business advisors that I come across have neither a professional qualification nor have run a successful business.

The beauty of having this external support, if you can find the right person, is that they can view your business more objectively than you and they have the benefit of the view from the bridge instead of the engine room.

As a qualified athletics coach I use a variety of techniques when training my athletes but the business world seems to separate these into four main strands. In practice there is a lot of overlap but they are broadly distinguished as:

- Coaches – use a number of techniques to help you find the right answer for yourself. Their expertise (and qualification) is in asking questions so do not expect them to have any knowledge of your industry. They will often challenge your thinking which can be uncomfortable for some business owners who are used to being the expert but it is worth it to start seeing things in a different way.
- Mentors – have expertise in your industry. They may use coaching techniques but they will also be able to provide some suggestions from their own experience. On the other hand some mentors lack the discipline of a coach and can only tell their own story, which may limit you.
- Consultants – have a particular area of expertise such as sales, marketing or software and would usually work with you on a project basis.

- Business advisors – these are usually people who have run businesses of some sort. Some are accountants who can analyse and advise on a structural basis, others are just retired business folk with variable success so do check out what they think you can learn from them.

The best way to choose who to work with is to be clear what sort of support you need. When I ran my accountancy business I worked with an excellent coach who was not an accountant but had coached many other accountants so I didn't have to waste time explaining a lot of the issues and jargon. Her personal expertise was in building teams and people issues which, as an introvert, was my own weak point. The right coach can help your business to come along in leaps and bounds.

Building your board

You may already have fellow directors but, as you grow, you will need to grow your management team based on skills and experience, but you may appoint your board based on other strengths too.

Functions that you may need on your board:

- Managing director/CEO
- Sales
- Marketing
- Finance
- HR
- Logistics
- Manufacturing
- IT
- Legal
- Operations

Depending on the size of the business that you are aiming for, then six to 12 is the maximum number for constructive meetings. If you do not have the expertise on your board then it can come from elsewhere in the company, at manager level or from an external consultant.

It is often assumed that the founder will become the CEO but if this is not your area of expertise then you might prefer to play to your own strengths and appoint an experienced business person to this role instead.

Companies with more diverse boards have been demonstrated to produce better results. This makes sense as people from different backgrounds, and with different experiences, can offer more ideas than a group of clones all repeating the same ideas.

Non-exec directors are not responsible for the day-to-day running of the company but can bring in expertise and experience on a part-time basis that you do not require, or cannot afford, on a full-time basis. As they are one step removed from the business they can often see things that are missed in the intensity of keeping everything functioning.

Solicitor

Ideally the business world would work on handshake commitments and completely clear agreements but, unfortunately, this is not the reality. Setting aside those who deliberately go back on their word or feel that they can operate outside the law there is still plenty of scope for misunderstandings.

When appointing somebody to a 'full-time' job, how many hours per week is full time? Where will they work? What constitutes doing a good job?

When paying 'on completion' of a piece of work you may need to define completion. Is content writing complete when the first draft is submitted or when the final, polished article is published? What if the client changes their mind and the article is never published? How many sets of edits are included in the price?

Right from the start it is easiest if any agreements are written down rather than verbal. Follow up important conversations with a confirmation email or similar. As soon as possible get everything drawn up professionally to minimise any elements of confusion.

A solicitor can help you with:

- Shareholder or partnership agreements to define what happens if one owner wants to sell, do less work or has a change in circumstances such as death or divorce
- Employment contracts
- Terms and conditions of sale (and payment!)

Choosing a solicitor

- Solicitor is a regulated title but lawyer is not.
- Ask for recommendations from your business colleagues and also ask why they like their solicitor. Mine is great because they speak plain English.
- Like accountants, solicitors will offer a free initial meeting so use

this to check that you get along. You need to be confident that they understand the requirements of you and your business.

Marketing expertise

First you need a strategy and then you may need several campaigns using a series of experts to implement them. Depending on your particular strategy you might need website designers, social media management, graphic design, advertising expertise (online or offline), copywriting, proofreading (please! It is almost impossible to proofread your own content and typos distract from the message) and website designers

Graphic designer and branding experts

We all want to get our businesses up and running as fast as possible and often don't have the time or finance to pay for a graphic designer. We need a quick logo before we really know what our business is about. I've described in Chapter 10 how our designer replaced my Times New Roman H with the more attractive bean design, a new name and a strapline. I had set up using blue as my brand colour, not because it is supposed to be synonymous with professionalism but because it is my favourite colour but the exact shade varied. My designer pinned us down to a particular blue plus a couple of complementary colours.

My current logo is an owl (symbol of wisdom) but have you noticed the plus sign in the tail as a hint at my numeracy? The blue has made way for teal which allows me to use any of my legacy blue dresses and stationery alongside it.

Now is the time to undergo a proper branding exercise to be clear about your business to your customers and prospects, and also your expanding team.

- Who is your market?
- What are your products and services?
- What is your USP (unique selling point) or why should customers buy from you instead of your competitors?
- What are your values?
- What do you help people to do or what problems do you solve?

All this can then be encompassed in a simple logo, business name and strapline which capture the core identity of your business.

Website designer

Yes, most of us can knock up a quick website on a WordPress template but, going forwards, you probably need something more representative of your growing brand in terms of functionality, visuals and professionally written content. Although I am an 'award-winning author' who gets paid to write content for others I am unable to write my own marketing content. It is hard to find the line between overselling yourself and being too humble but an external content writer can see the balance more easily.

IT

Hardware, software, telecommunications: all are essential to most businesses and, when they go wrong, they can really upset the smooth running of the work. When tools don't work properly you have people unable to do their job and productivity as well as morale will drop.

In order to scale up you need to ensure that your systems are kept up to date, properly supported and secure. It's time to review your approach to IT as well as the actual systems you are using.

It is probably the time to add some expertise to your team if you haven't already. You have now moved beyond spending hours fiddling around to try and fix something yourself and need to call in the experts by way of an outsourced maintenance contract or an in-house expert. IT can seem like a black box of things which can go wrong so make sure that you find somebody not just competent to look after your existing systems, but who can understand the requirements of your business.

It's not just your hardware maintenance. You should look for a software expert (often an app integrator who can connect different software systems together) who should be able to suggest alternative software which will help you to grow your business with confidence.

IT can be key to scaling up by automating some of the work.

Sarah's story

Sarah ran a professional services company and, on my recommendation, introduced a particular piece of workflow management software which would automate some of their administrative work and improve communications within the team too. The team had spare capacity now that they were not wasting time on admin.

First Sarah used their time to delegate the last of her 'hands-on' work so that she had a day a week to work on her business. She also freed up sufficient time to achieve her personal goal of playing golf twice a month with clients and introducers (and reduced her golf handicap in the process).

Sarah benefited financially when a staff member left and did not need to be replaced as the rest of the team were able to absorb his workload due to this and some additional automation.

Then Sarah had a crisis when one of her team was suddenly taken ill and out of action for a few weeks. This is where the documentation came into play as Sarah and the rest of the team were able to pick up the urgent parts of their team-mate's work and ensure that this was covered to a suitable standard. The only negative was that Sarah didn't get to play her two games of golf that month but she made sure that she was back out on the course the following month.

Insurance

Public liability, professional indemnity, employer's liability, property and motor insurance are essential from the start but you might want to look at covering additional risks. Once you are dependent on your business for a healthy income you might choose sickness benefits, medical cover or key man insurance to help in the event that you or another vital member of your team are unable to work. Different insurances can pay to get the individual back to work faster with private healthcare, cover the cost of a temporary replacement or even make up any lost earnings. Call in a broker to assess your needs and to find you a good deal.

Financial advisor

Once your business is successful you will want to maximise your personal lifetime income through profits and eventual sale. While you will probably reinvest at least some of your profits into the business you might also want to set aside some of your hard-earned cash in the form of a pension. A pension is a tax-efficient wrapper for all sorts of investments. While part of your pension may come from the sale of your business it is wise to consider spreading the risk across other investments too.

Calling in the professionals requires a change of mindset. You should aim to only be doing the things which *only* you can do. Not only will this free up your time to focus on what you do best but you will usually find that experts will be so much better that they will produce much more value than they cost.

The numbers to watch

- 'If you think using a professional is expensive you should try using an amateur.' Hopefully you will never experience the damages and costs of using an amateur who doesn't know what they are doing or takes an exceptionally long time to do it.

Summary

Types of external expert you might call in are:

- Accountant
- Bookkeeper
- Coach, mentor, business advisor
- Marketing consultant
- Marketing experts for branding, graphic design, content writing, social media management, advertising, printing, web design, PR, events organisation, etc.
- Solicitor
- IT support team
- Insurance broker
- Health and safety expert
- HR consultant

Chapter 16

Buying a business

16. Buying a business

Buying a business is one way to grow your business quickly rather than the slow process of growing organically. It may also be something to consider if you wish to break into a certain field.

Pros of buying:

- Grow your business faster than you would organically
- Roll out your successful processes to a larger market
- Economies of scale
- Move into a new area, geographically or by acquiring new techniques or products
- Buy out a competitor

Cons of buying:

- Cost
- Time taken to integrate new business and staff
- Time taken for handover and to reassure new clients, some of whom will dislike any changes, even for the good
- The new business may have different ways of working so clients have a different expectation
- Buying somebody else's problem clients/jobs as the previous owner may not have been as diligent as you in improving or moving these along
- Depending on the nature of the business and acquisition you may encounter all of the problems of new customers all at the same time

Finding a business to buy

Dalton's directory (www.daltonsbusiness.com) is a good place to find small businesses advertised for sale.

Your accountant or solicitor may well know of, or can enquire about, local businesses for sale.

There are specialist brokers dealing with the buying and selling of businesses and it is usually the buyer who pays their fees. They can proactively search for you. The agent will provide you with a shortlist of businesses to buy, showing such things as:

- Turnover
- A broad outline of the business
- Number of staff

- Whether premises are available
- Whether the business is portable to another office/location
- Once you have signed a non-disclosure agreement (NDA) you will be able to see:
- Previous years' accounts and management accounts
- Customer details
- Organisation chart or other staff details

This is the stage at which you would probably meet the vendor.

Why acquisitions don't proceed

When I first set up my business I was constantly on the lookout for a suitable company to buy and I had preliminary talks with a few. These are some of the reasons why an acquisition might not proceed beyond the enquiry stage:

- Mismatch on requirements to retain staff and premises.
- Mismatch in IT systems means additional work to integrate.
- Mismatch in clients means that they are not desirable or they would take additional work to integrate.
- Mismatch in the way the existing owners work with their clients, meaning that they will not adapt to a new owner.
- Business sale may force a member of staff to leave and clients may follow them instead of staying with the new owner.
- Retiring owners are still hands on and the business is not sufficiently profitable to cover the costs of employing somebody to carry out their work and also cover the repayments and interest on any necessary finance.
- The business may well be past the point where it can be saved if the previous owner has been winding down for retirement rather than actively preparing the business for sale.
- Mismatch in pricing if retiring owners have not increased fees for some time.
- Retiring owners aren't really ready to retire and hand over.
- Retiring owners overvalue their business for any reason.

Some of these issues can be overcome by adjusting the purchase price but, for others, it is best to walk away.

I did find one accountancy practice which was beautifully prepared for sale by the part-time owner but I eventually, and reluctantly, concluded that it was slightly too far away to fit with either my current marketing strategy or my family commitments. This one was really difficult to turn down and I kept having to come back to my little notebook with my primary business purpose.

How much should you pay?

How long is a piece of string?

There are a number of ways to value businesses and so I would refer you to any of the books on the subject or get a valuation via your accountant.

Here are some general rules:

- Three to five times historical annual net profit.
- Make sure that the profit is adjusted to include a salary for any retiring shareholder/directors who are currently receiving most of their remuneration via dividends. If they are still hands on you will need to replace all or part of their role with a suitably qualified person, or to backfill your own position while you take over some of their work. It may be a good idea to take on additional resources for the transition period anyway.

Net assets

Don't just use their current book value from the accounts. These should be adjusted at their value to you. If you don't need all the equipment then it may only be worth scrap value to you. Debtors need to be adjusted for irrecoverable amounts.

Goodwill

This is often the value of things like the brand and intellectual property.

Things that will affect this valuation:

- If you plan to make any changes to premises, staffing and processes these should be reflected in your calculations of what the business is worth to you.
- How good a fit the business is for you and how quickly you can integrate both businesses. Remember that any changes may disturb both customers and staff so the speed at which you progress is a fine balance.
- If the business will run independently of the retiring owner due to the systems in place and well-trained staff.
- The nature of the clients and their loyalty to the brand rather than the retiring owner or any staff who may move on to competitors.

Other contract factors

- Payment period. Some payment will be required immediately but the balance may be paid over a longer period. While this will reduce your need for external finance it may also increase the price that you pay.
- If the vendors are required to stay on for a while to ensure a smooth handover this may be at an agreed salary or part of the price may be based on future profitability. This gives a financial incentive to the seller to ensure a smooth handover. It may be that the vendor wants to be certain of their financial position and will accept a lower fixed price so that the risk is with you, the purchaser.
- Non-compete clause. There will be a period during which the seller cannot act against the interests of the business by offering an alternative product/service to their former clients either directly or while working for somebody else. This must be a reasonable restriction overall but it is helpful to find out what your seller intends to do afterwards to ensure that there is no conflict between their old and new work. They should not be allowed to approach existing clients or staff for a period either, although this is always hard to enforce where friendships are involved.

Other considerations

As part of the due diligence process you need to check:

- the accounts and the assets that you are buying
- that the customer, supplier, staff and other contracts are in place
- a sample of the products or services and so on
- any written procedures (or try to observe what is different from your own business)
- the contract itself.

On the day of the sale you should receive:

- Keys
- Passwords
- Customer contracts
- Supplier contracts
- Staff contracts
- Procedures manuals
- Anything else that you need to run the business

Legals

I would recommend using a solicitor in the process. They will ensure that there are guarantees in the contract if you make discoveries post sale that did not come to light as part of your due diligence checks. You will also want to put in place some sort of non-compete clause restricting your vendor from competing against you directly or via a third party. There may be other restrictions that you wish to put in place concerning poaching both clients and staff.

Insurance

You need to ensure that insurance is in place from day one and, as soon as possible, reissue contracts in the name of the new company. If you are buying the shares of the company then you have longer to arrange to transfer bank accounts. As an attempt to smooth the handover in both my acquisition and sale, the buyer was appointed director prior to the final sale. There is, of course, a risk with this. We tried to set up the new bank signatory beforehand too but your vendor might prefer to wait until after the sale. Any leases and so on may need to be transferred into the buyer's name.

Share or asset purchase

This process is all much simpler if you are buying the shares in the company; however, you will also be taking on all the assets and liabilities of the business too. A share sale is simpler as the bank accounts and office lease will be in the company name. This allows you to transfer everything at your convenience. The alternative is to arrange to transfer all contracts and insurances on the day of sale.

You and the vendor will also want to consider the tax aspects of each type of transfer in your particular circumstances. Your accountant will be able to advise on this.

Meeting the team

The other thing that you will probably want to do early on is to speak to the staff. The business that I bought had three subcontractors. My preference was to employ my team and so, when telling them about the acquisition, I offered them all employed positions. One took me up on this offer and the other two preferred to remain as subcontractors. We arranged a dinner in a local pub so that both teams could meet and get to know each other.

Taking on more staff meant that we were bursting at the seams in our existing office (even with storing most of the marketing materials, stationery and archiving off site) so I had to find larger premises in a hurry. Do build this into your expansion plans as it took us nearly six months to find and refurbish a suitable office space.

Handover

As part of the acquisition you should expect a period of two to 12 months post sale for the seller to make all necessary introductions and to generally smooth the way. Any work during and after this handover period may be in the seller's interest if there is an earn-out clause, which means that part of the sale price is based on the future profitability of the new business, but it would be normal to pay a salary or consultancy fee for any material work.

It is important that you take the time to find a company which is a good fit for your business as this will help clients to settle into the new regime more easily and they will be more likely to stay with you. You and the seller will need to identify key clients to visit or at least telephone to make personal introductions. These visits may be made before the sale takes place or, if it is kept quiet for commercial reasons, immediately afterwards.

For the remaining 'new' clients and any introducers and suppliers, you will need to agree a suitable letter of introduction with the vendor. The emphasis should be on business as usual but, if there are to be changes in staff or location, this should be made clear and the benefits explained to the clients. You may wish to let your existing clients know what is happening too.

When I sold my own business we held a reception to give all existing clients an opportunity to meet the buyer informally but also gave them the option of more formal business meetings during the daytime. This was a good way to ensure that everybody was looked after as it was impossible to arrange to personally visit all clients beforehand.

Publicity

Buying a business provides a good opportunity to raise your profile with a press release.

Avoiding pitfalls

With the benefit of hindsight I would prefer to grow organically rather than by acquisition because:

- in integrating new clients and systems I was unable to focus on growing the business organically – with so many new clients coming on board at once I was quite exhausted trying to manage it all as quickly as possible
- in buying another business you are inheriting different problems and client expectations that you would normally filter out at the initial meeting stage.

If you are not confident in your ability to grow organically, then you should certainly consider growth by acquisition. It is also a good way to acquire new skills or products that you don't have in your current business.

The numbers to watch

- Profitability for the last three years
- Inflation-adjusted profit forecasts
- Net assets

Summary

Things to consider when buying a business are:

- Finding a good fit
- Agreeing the price
- Agreeing payment terms
- Share acquisition or net assets
- Meeting the team
- Client handover
- Making the announcements

Chapter 17

Funding expansion

17. Funding expansion

Whether buying a business or growing organically, there may be times when you need additional funds. There are a number of sources that you can access directly or with the help of your accountant.

Grants

Grants are often available to purchase equipment, expand overseas, create jobs or for coaching that will allow you to scale up. There are also grants for certain regions or industries.

The details of these change on a regular basis and many were funded by the EU but they are usually there in some form. Your local chamber of commerce is a good place to enquire about these.

Many of these grants will require you to pay out first and then reclaim some or all of the money. This is not very helpful in terms of cash flow but the promise of future income can help you to get short-term funding elsewhere.

You may require an independent financial review (not a statutory audit) by a suitably qualified accountant of your claim before funds are released.

Banks

Banks will often lend for business growth but they will not lend to cover losses. In order to access finance you will need to prepare a business plan and cash flow forecast detailing exactly how you will repay the money and the interest and when. Rates are cheaper if they are secured on an asset. You will need to provide regular financial updates.

Hire purchase or other supplier finance

This is usually secured on the asset that you are purchasing and is an incentive for you to buy when you may not otherwise be able to afford it. In this case prepare a business plan and cash flow forecast so that you know that you can afford it.

Invoice financing

Selling your debts is very useful to get a one-off influx of cash. Some companies will buy the debt off you completely and take on the debt collection themselves; you may still have to repay the amount advanced if there turns out to be a bad debt. Other companies will expect you to collect the debt and repay them the advance.

Asset-based finance and mortgages

Funding is more easily available if the loan can be secured on an asset or a property as this is more secure for the lender than relying on future profits. In this case prepare a business plan and cash flow forecast so that you know that you can afford it.

Venture capitalists (VCs)

These will be prepared to take higher risks. They will often base their decision on investing in the individuals as much as the business itself. They will probably expect to take a share of the company in return for that risk. VCs will reap their reward when the company is sold. If you do not wish to sell your business you will need to have the means to buy them out at the future market rate. VC funding often comes with expertise which should ensure the success of the venture.

Even if the finance is on the basis of a loan they will probably take shares as a security in the event that the loan is not repaid. You will need to provide regular updates on the progress of your plan.

Crowdfunding

This is where you get a lot of small investors to finance you. There may well be an incentive, for instance one client crowdfunded her book by promising copies for all her investors. It was a very sophisticated way of making advance sales. These campaigns are more successful if a chunk of the funding has already been secured in advance.

Personal savings

It is in your interests to prepare a business plan and cash flow forecast so that you know that you will be repaid. Too often personal insolvencies follow the insolvency of a small business.

The numbers to watch

- Amount required
- Interest rate
- Payment terms and cash flow impact
- Consider the worst-case scenario as well as the most likely

Summary

- Nobody, except maybe your family, will invest to cover losses.
- If you can offer security then you should receive a lower interest rate.
- Be prepared to provide three years' accounts, up-to-date management accounts and a business plan showing repayment and cash flow.
- Lenders will be reassured if the business owner understands the numbers, not just the accountant.
- Lenders will be reassured if all management accounts, etc. are readily available.

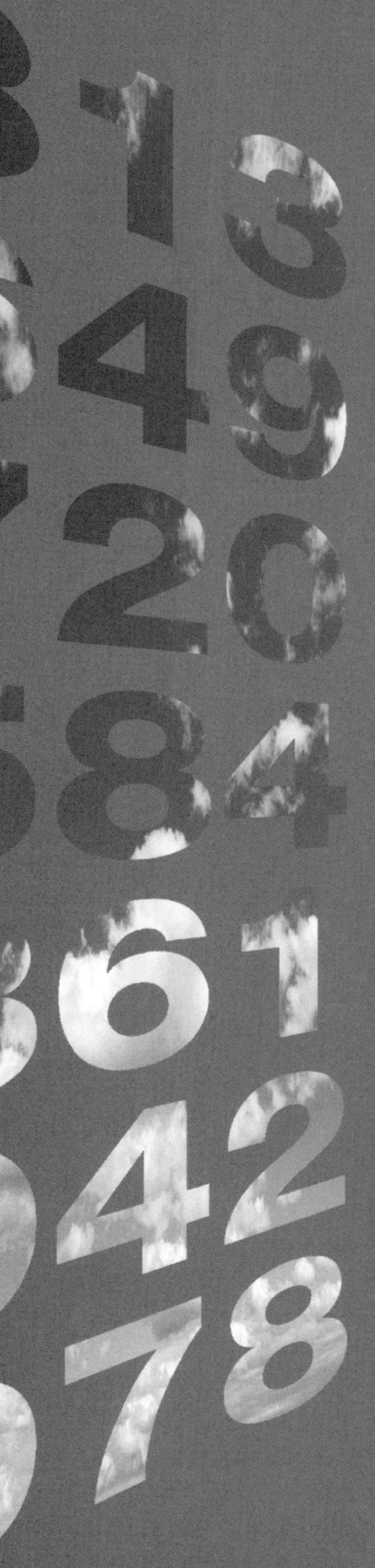

Chapter 18

Doing business for good

18. Doing business for good

I have always believed in contributing to the local community but have also found it a very good way to promote the business and to provide a lot of job satisfaction.

Pros of community work:

- Increased profile in the community, some of which is with other local businesses
- Creating referrers and ambassadors for the brand
- Identifying potential employees
- Helping others
- Improving the community in which you live/work
- Opportunities for PR articles
- Doing something you enjoy for the benefit of the community and your business

Cons of community work:

- Cost compared to uncertain returns
- Scattergun approach to marketing as much of it falls outside your target prospects
- Time spent in carrying out activities is non-fee earning

Issues to consider

There are a number of ways to contribute to the local community and some will be more appealing than others. As an owner-managed business you may decide that personal satisfaction offsets some of the time/cost involved. For instance, my love of sport meant that I was happy to sponsor local grassroots and charity football matches with a low chance of commercial reward. I was fortunate that most of these did reap financial benefits.

There are several ways that you might choose to 'pay it forward'.

Commercial karma

Helping others through referrals and introductions costs you nothing but, if you introduce the right people, it generates a great deal of goodwill from both parties from the introduction. For this reason you might want to be careful who you introduce. Sometimes I make qualified introductions to people who share the same values along the lines of 'I haven't done business with them but they are good people so please let me know how you get on.'

Some of the closed networking groups encourage such referrals but focus more on quantity than quality. If you are a member of such a group you should get to know your fellow members and exactly how they can (or can't) help your contacts. A poor referral wastes everybody's time and reflects badly on you. In this type of group you should also be clear what makes a good referral for you. When we stopped doing tax for individuals and introduced a minimum fee we still received enquiries from referrers who didn't know this. Even now, two years after selling my accountancy business, I still get people approaching me about doing their accounts.

Do not expect reciprocal referrals; this is primarily about helping others but it will generate goodwill in the business community as a whole.

I often volunteer my time when ICAEW requires business advisors. It's something that I enjoy doing as I love helping people to grow their businesses. After years of doing this I was invited to chair the ICAEW practice conference in London. One of the other speakers there heard me and passed on a referral when another speaker dropped out of a different conference. It turned out that the conference organisers organised 18 other events throughout the year and invited me to speak. Needless to say, I agreed, but I also suggested three other good speakers who would enhance those conferences. None of this was done with the aim of benefiting myself but I have been amply rewarded as a result.

Helping schools

When helping schools you are in a position both to mould what they do in order to generate more useful employees in the future and also to talent-spot individuals whom you might wish to employ yourself. As a parent I'm keen to think that others, in turn, will do this for my children.

The things that I have done include:

- Mock interviews. They usually follow a pattern prescribed by the school.
- Work experience. You will need to have a risk assessment for young people and employee liability insurance but your local council will help with the formalities. We provided a mixture of work projects requiring a little learning and then minimal supervision. I also took our students along to a couple of networking events and client meetings. Do get permission from the event organiser and your client beforehand! I arranged for all students to sign our confidentiality contract. While not enforceable in law it served as a reminder to them of the importance of confidentiality in our profession. Work experience can also act as an extended interview and I found a great apprentice in this way.

- Careers fairs. We prepared for these in the same way as for business/ trade fairs. There is no charge to exhibit and you have the opportunity to talk to lots of potential recruits about accountancy or starting a business in general. Most of these are accompanied by parents who may themselves be part of your target market so it helps to increase your profile in the wider community. We provided goody bags with our name on that we hoped reminded others of us for a while longer.
- Careers talks. I love what I do and so I love telling kids all about my work, my training and all the routes open to them with each type and level of accountancy qualification. These days I can also talk to them about running my own business and writing an award-winning business book.
- Business games. These are usually organised by ICAEW or Young Enterprise. Untrained youngsters often have a fresh way of looking at the world that we can all learn from. This variety of world views is why businesses benefit from diversity in gender, age, ethnicity, etc. as they produce a rainbow of ideas rather than the monochrome suggestions that might come from a group of people just like you.

Charity pro bono and how to say no (and yes)

A quick online search shows that there are over 35 charities and community groups in our village. All of these require a treasurer and some need an independent review.

There may be particular charities that appeal to your heart or your interests so prioritise these. Spending five hours counting cash after a school parent–teacher association event may not feel like the best use of your time and expertise but it provides a clear role model for your own children.

In addition I set aside a budget for pro bono work. The idea was that we would charge commercial fees for the work (we are not a charity after all, and still need to pay staff and bills) but would subsidise part or all of the fee from the pro bono budget. When the budget was gone I would explain this and also that, as the budget was a percentage of our fees, we could give more as the business grew. This made it easy to say 'no' while also pointing out the link that we could give more if we received more.

Sponsorship

I love sport, especially grassroots sport, so I loved contributing to local football and rugby clubs and a few charity events. The commercial benefits from each club/ event included our name on advertising boards, shirts, programmes, websites and so on. The clubs also provided opportunities for PR in local publications and some arranged networking events or lunches for sponsors.

I found this a great way of combining business and pleasure so I was always nicely surprised when we picked up new clients as a result. It was definitely an opportunity to meet people with similar interests, which led to these new clients, so do go along and be seen at the club/event so that you are more than just an anonymous advert.

By sponsoring events or groups that you enjoy it will feel like so much more than just an overhead. Business should be enjoyable whenever possible.

Always check what benefits you will receive in exchange for your sponsorship and make sure that these match your personal requirements too. Some sports sponsorship provides an opportunity to meet your favourite players.

Do you have useful facilities?

Small businesses and networking groups need meeting space. If you have unused training or meeting rooms you can allow clients and other business groups to use these for their own meetings.

One training client regularly brought growing businesses into our premises for their events and the only cost to us was tea, coffee and biscuits. This was exactly our target market and we didn't have to do anything more than put the kettle on.

We also hosted events for the local chamber of commerce. These were events which I would have attended anyway but they allowed us to increase our profile in the local business community. We only had to provide basic refreshments or a few additional items at cost.

Do you get discounts when purchasing items which you can allow community groups to share if they need to purchase similar items?

Collaboration

For a couple of years I belonged to a formal collaboration group of non-local accountants. As we were not in direct competition we helped each other out with ideas and what had or hadn't worked for us. I received lots of help from others in the group when we introduced services or software that they had already tried and I hope that they gained as much from me. I still keep in touch with them along with others in an informal network. I also host similar groups myself now as 'retreats' for business owners to focus on their business while supported by other business owners who will happily share their ideas.

I was always keen to have coffee with other local accountants to see where we could help each other and also, exactly, where we were in competition. As we were too small to provide every single service that clients might want, I believe in referring enquiries to the best accountant for the client and this wasn't always us. We didn't do tax for individuals and we were not cost effective for the smallest, lifestyle businesses. At the other end of the scale we did not always have the specialist knowledge that certain businesses needed so it was right to refer them to others whom we knew and trusted.

Similarly you can limit your stock holdings if you focus on your best sellers and are prepared to refer elsewhere or come to an arrangement with a 'competitor' so that you don't both have to hold on to slow-moving items.

Ethics

While we may have had to sign up to the ethics of our professional and trade bodies, there are broader decisions to make in how we operate our businesses.

My elderly marketing lecturer at university summed it up when he told all us keen youngsters that business ethics are often subjective so we should decide for ourselves what we considered right and wrong and then stick to it. We may all differ on exactly where we draw the line on certain issues. I assume that you would never support tax evasion but how do you stand on advanced tax planning? Do you question your accountant when a tax 'scheme' sounds too good to be true or are you comfortable turning a blind eye? Be very clear on what you will and won't do and never change this just because you are desperate to keep a customer.

Avoiding pitfalls

- Decide in advance how much time/money you are prepared to pay for things with little direct commercial benefit but other rewards such as showing corporate social responsibility (CSR) or just being a responsible business.
- Do not be sucked into taking on too much pro bono work in the hope that it will lead to something more; it usually doesn't.
- Remember that some charities can afford to pay for your services so save your pro bono work for others which can't.
- It is OK to say 'no'.
- Always invoice your charities even if you show a 100 per cent discount so that they appreciate the value of your services.

The numbers to watch

- It's very hard to track how helping one group of people seems to lead to additional business further down the line but there is a clear correlation that the more good I do along the way, the more successful my business. It may be commercial karma or it may just be an improved reputation in the business world

- Discounts given for charity or community work
- Time spent volunteering
- Various statistics for diversity and gender pay gap even if your business is not yet big enough for this to be a legal requirement

Summary

- Work out the benefits you will definitely receive for your time/cash.
- Work out the benefits you will possibly receive for your time/cash.
- Some of these benefits may not be purely commercial.
- Assess your ROI on each activity.
- Some charities/community causes may be more appealing to you than others; you are free to choose, subject to any other shareholders and finance arrangements.
- You can, and should, say 'no' to things which do not satisfy you financially or that do not fit with your values as the business owner.

Conclusion

Running a business is hard and it is not for everyone so congratulations on getting this far with your dream.

As the owner, the buck stops with you, so surround yourself with a supportive network in your business life and home life.

Systemise your business as much as possible to make your own life easier – these systems are the key to expanding and to eventually selling the business.

Never undervalue yourself. You have brought your business this far so you clearly have a good product/service and loyal customers.

Charge enough to provide the agreed service level.

- The next steps that you might take as a result of reading this book:
- Write your Big Business Plan and grow your business by working through this book and other resources such as the Growing by Numbers online course or business coaching.
- Focus on one tricky area by using some of the Further resources in the next section of this book.
- Decide that you are happy with the current size of your business after all and just use the ideas in this book, perhaps with some of our business coaching, to tweak the bits you need to run more efficiently or profitably or to give you a better work/life balance.

Whatever you do, enjoy the ride and do let me know how you're getting on or if you have any good news to share: GBN@hudsonbusiness.co.uk.

Further resources

Hudson Business resources

I have mentioned a number of our own resources. You can find further information by registering your copy of the book at GBN@hudsonbusiness.co.uk.

Our resources include:

- Finance for Business Owners webinar
- Business valuation spreadsheet
- Retirement forecast spreadsheet
- Goal-setting webinars
- Strategic planning day
- Pricing webinar
- Hourly rate calculation spreadsheet
- Growing by Numbers online course
- Business coaching (group and individual)
- Retreats for business owners to take time out to focus on their business
- Balanced 10 webinar
- Five-year plan template

Chapter 1, Understanding your accounts

- Hudson Business, Finance for Business Owners webinar

Chapter 2, Deciding your exit strategy

- Hudson Business, Business valuation spreadsheet
- Hudson Business, Retirement forecast spreadsheet
- Budd, Chris (2018) *The Eternal Business: How to transition a business for the employee ownership revolution.* Harriman House Publishing
- Sale of business assets versus shares: http://ukbusinessbrokers.com/asset-sale-vs-share-sale-whats-better-deal/
- Entrepreneurs' Relief

Chapter 3, Your accounting toolbox

- Hudson Business, Goal-setting webinars
- Hudson Business, Strategic planning day
- Budd, Chris (2016) *The Financial Wellbeing Book: Creating Financial Peace of Mind (Concise Advice).* LID Publishing

Chapter 4, Non-financial KPIs

- Hudson Business, Finance for Business Owners webinar

Chapter 5, Setting your prices

- Hudson Business, Pricing webinar
- Hudson Business, Hourly rate calculation spreadsheet

Chapter 6, Budgeting and controlling costs

- Hudson Business, Budget spreadsheet

Chapter 7, Reviewing your systems and services

- Gerber, Michael E. (2001) *The E-Myth Revisited: Why most small businesses don't work and what to do about it.* HarperBusiness
- Hudson Business, Growing by Numbers online course
- Hudson Business, Business coaching (group and individual)
- Hudson Business, Retreats for business owners to take time out to focus on their business

Chapter 8, Building and retaining your team

- SMART Support for Business – outsourced appraisals and DISC profiling
- Hudson Business, Balanced 10 webinar

Chapter 9, Moving into premises

- Claiming use of home: www.gov.uk/expenses-if-youre-self-employed
- Principal Private Residence Relief: www.gov.uk/tax-sell-home

Chapter 10, Marketing your business

- Thomas, Bryony (2020) *Watertight Marketing: The Proven Process for Seriously Scaleable Sales.* Human Business Thinking, and Watertight Marketing training and consulting
- Valuable content: www.valuablecontent.co.uk
- Digital Mums: www.digitalmums.com
- Professional Speaking Association: www.thepsa.co.uk
- Eventbrite: www.eventbrite.co.uk
- Hootsuite, social media scheduling software: www.hootsuite.com
- Active Campaign CRM software: www.activecampaign.com
- Smarter queue, social media scheduling software

Chapter 11, Basic bookkeeping

- Hudson Business, Finance for Business Owners webinar
- Xero accounting software
- QuickBooks Online accounting software
- FreeAgent accounting software
- iZettle card reader: www.izettle.com/gb
- Square card reader: www.squareup.com/gb
- GoCardless for online payments and direct debits: www.gocardless.com
- Chaser.io for chasing invoices: www.chaserhq.com
- Receipt Bank for taking the pain out of invoice entry: www.receipt-bank.com
- Hubdoc for taking the pain out of invoice entry: www.hubdoc.com
- Autoentry for taking the pain out of invoice entry: www.autoentry.com
- Expensify for taking the pain out of invoice entry: www.expensify.com
- DEAR warehouse management systems: www.dearsystems.com
- Zapier for connecting systems: www.zapier.com
- Workato for connecting systems: www.workato.com
- Stripe for online card payments: www.stripe.com/gb
- Clover point of sale software and card reader: www.clover.com
- Shopify for ecommerce: www.shopify.com
- Harvest time-tracking and expenses: www.getharvest.com
- Workflow Max project management: www.workflowmax.com
- Spotlight reporting and forecasting: www.spotlightreporting.com
- Futrli reporting and forecasting: www.futrli.com
- Fluidly cash flow forecasting: www.fluidly.com
- Float cash flow forecasting: www.floatapp.com

Chapter 12, The language of accounts

- Hudson Business, Finance for Business Owners webinar

Chapter 13, Writing a business plan

- Hudson Business, Five-year plan template
- Hudson Business, Strategic planning day

Chapter 14, Controlling your cash flow

- Fluidly cash flow forecasting: www.fluidly.com
- Float cash flow forecasting: www.floatapp.com
- Chaser.io for chasing invoices: www.chaserhq.com

Chapter 15, Calling in the professionals

- FSB for employment law, tax advice and assorted legal contracts: www.fsb.org.uk
- ICAEW, Institute of Chartered Accountants of England and Wales: www.icaew.com
- ACCA, Chartered Association of Certified Accountants: www.accaglobal.com
- CIMA, Chartered Institute of Management Accountants: www.cimaglobal.com
- CIOT, Chartered Institute of Taxation: www.tax.org.uk
- AAT, Association of Accounting Technicians: www.aat.org.uk
- ICB, Institute of Certified Bookkeepers: www.bookkeepers.org.uk
- Hudson Business, Business coaching (group and individual)

Chapter 16, Buying a business

- Hudson Business, Business valuation spreadsheet

Chapter 17, Funding expansion

- British Business Angels Association: www.ukbaa.org.uk

Chapter 18, Doing business for good

- B1G1 Business for Good: www.b1g1.com/businessforgood

About the author

Della Hudson has been working in accountancy since 1989, when she first started training as a chartered accountant after completing her degree in chemistry and management at City, University of London. Apart from a brief spell in IT she spent most of her career working in industry and helping to run UK subsidiaries of large multinationals.

In 2009, with two small children to look after, Della set up her own chartered accountancy practice, Hudson Business Accountants and Advisers, on her kitchen table and grew it to a team of eight people in independent offices before selling up in 2017.

With no thoughts of retiring, Della now works as a speaker, writer and business coach to all sorts of businesses alongside her non-executive director and finance director roles. Her first book, *The Numbers Business: how to grow a successful cloud accountancy practice* won the specialist book category at the 2019 Business Book Awards 2019 and became an Amazon bestseller. She then went on to co-author the Bloomsbury *Tax Planning 2019/20* guide and finally impressed her teenage kids by sharing the same publisher as their beloved J.K. Rowling. Della was even shortlisted as the ICB personality of the year 2019; quite an achievement for a Hufflepuff.

In her free time Della enjoys the swim/bike/run of triathlons and cooking and eating with friends.